JUSTIN FATICA

HARD AS NAILS

A MISSION TO AWAKEN YOUTH TO THE POWER OF GOD'S LOVE

Image Books   Doubleday

New York   London   Toronto   Sydney   Auckland

Published in the United States by Doubleday, an imprint of The
Doubleday Publishing Group, a division of Random House,
Inc., New York
www.doubleday.com

IMAGE, DOUBLEDAY, and the portrayal of a deer drinking from a
stream are registered trademarks of Random House, Inc.

The source for the biblical quotes is the *New American Bible*
(or the NAB), which is used by the Catholic Church.

Library of Congress Cataloging-in-Publication Data

Fatica, Justin.
Hard as nails / by Justin Fatica. — 1st ed.
p. cm.
1. Fatica, Justin. 2. Hard as Nails Ministries—
Biography. 3. Catholics—United States—
Biography. 4. Church work with youth—Catholic
Church. 5. Church work with youth—United States. I. Title.
BX4705.F2627A3 2009
259'.23—dc22
2008019765

ISBN 978-0-385-52717-0

PRINTED IN THE UNITED STATES OF AMERICA

3 5 7 9 10 8 6 4 2

To the women in my life who have taught me to be compassionate and to love all people:

For my beautiful wife, Mary Fatica, who has shown me what is important in life; she is my lighthouse in a dark world.

For my precious mother, Kathleen Fatica, who has provided me with love and stability through all of my life challenges.

For my grandmother Anne Iverson, who has loved me unconditionally no matter what.

For my grandmother Carmelina "Millie" Fatica, who has been a bold witness to her Catholic faith and her love for Mary the Mother of God and the Church.

Contents

A Poem for Joseph

To my firstborn son,

I lay awake thinking, praying, and looking at you.

How can I touch and move the hearts of many adults and youth, not few?

They are coming at me by the hundreds, many hearts numb, hurt, and afraid.

How can I bear this burden for you, son? There is only one way—in the Lord Jesus's NAME!

Children committing suicide, parents leaving, boys and girls raped and molested, brothers shot dead and gone, good kids picked on, and many have gone astray.

The businessmen are making money. The crowds all run away. Hey, son, someone needs to face them, full-time without shame.

God says, "Come on, Daddy, don't be ashamed. Face them for your babies' future. I can help you. I understand the pain."

I sit and watch you, son. I cannot be afraid.

I am trying so hard and I am making mistakes along the way.

For every mother and father hurting inside because they feel they are losing their son or daughter,

For all young people who can't trust anybody because they don't even know their father,

I am crying now. Please listen to my heart.

Mr. and Mrs. Smith, Jones, Coleman, and even lonely Miss Mildred,

Every message I speak, I will remember your children.

All of them, all of them, Muslim, Jew, Hindu, Atheist, Catholics and Christians of all faiths, they are the future leaders of the world and will grow up to be men and women.

As my son lies asleep I pray and thank him for teaching me to love with all my heart and believe.

Even though there are a few adults who challenge me and think I am too extreme, I will not stop loving them with all

my heart until they understand that we need to all stop being mean.

I sit and watch you, son, as I pray. Oh please I hope it is
not too late.

A great-grandma just stopped me as I prayed.

She said, "Young man, love and love and do not be afraid."

Love, Your Daddy

Foreword by David Tyree

The first time I experienced Justin's Hard as Nails Ministries was when I saw the HBO documentary *Hard as Nails* in the fall of 2007. All I saw was this extremely passionate white guy wearing a jersey screaming about the love of Christ, so I had to fall back and see what it was all about. The next scene was him hammering the cross with some kids and I said to myself this is not your typical Catholic. The truth is there is no denomination in the Body of Christ. I thought this Justin must be spirit-filled and I enjoyed every bit of the documentary.

I finally met Justin the following April at a Syracuse University spring football game. Syracuse is my alma mater; I didn't know that he was living there. I already loved the fact that he was from Jersey and he loved the fact that I was totally sold on giving all the glory to Christ for what took place at Super Bowl XLII, when we beat the Patriots. We shared a lot in common as young men the Lord has trusted with building up young people in ministry. Both of us are very passionate about lifting the standard of Christ as the only way, truth, and life. He is a brother in the Spirit whom I admire and look up to for his boldness and lack of restraint when sharing the truth of God's love for us. Our relationship will grow and mature as we watch God's plan unfold for the ministry.

I believe that Justin can have a powerful impact not only in the sports arena but also on other people. Justin does not operate in fear, which is the major challenge for many believers. His interest in training and in athletics complements the gifts that God has already given him. There is no need to align the message of love and hope to the sports culture, but only to allow Christ to prevail in the ministry and let the Kingdom of God become part of the lives of athletes everywhere.

My story is too long for me to write completely here, but it includes alcohol addiction, selling and using marijuana, being sexually out there, etc. You could probably find articles all over the Internet about how Christ resurrected my life and gave me hope. Our young people have been stripped of their rightful inheritance as children of God. They are desperately searching for fulfillment in things but they are only spiraling down the path of destruction. Many are gripped with fear that they will not be accepted even though God made them who they are. They are searching for love and acceptance, only to be shunned by the coldness of the world. While searching for their identity, many young people enter into journeys of despair while searching for something pure and true. They are not acknowledging God because the local church has painted such a corrupt picture. The only thing pure, true, and perfect is the love of the Father through His son, Jesus Christ, but the glory is in Him using imperfect vessels like us to display His glory.

I'm trying to shake the religious cloak that society has

used to portray our faith. We must bring our young people back to the heart of the Father through His son, Jesus. God has given us, his children, authority, dominion, and power and I intend to teach, train, and activate a generation through the love of Jesus. It's a battle over which God has already declared victory but we must choose sides. Time out for the weak and the faint of heart but we fight the good fight of faith until Jesus cracks the sky and the light shines through! Victory is ours but we must do our part. In the sports world your life is your witness. I am my integrity but I'm free to be who God created me to be. I can't allow my goodness to be spoken of evilly and I don't walk around with a Bible and a microphone preaching. I try to hear God, to minister in his love, and to listen to the hearts of my fellow players, just like Justin's ministry does with young people every day.

David Tyree is currently a wide receiver with the New York Giants, winners of the 2008 Super Bowl. He caught the incredible helmet pass from Eli Manning during Super Bowl XLII (2008). He has recently started a local ministry for youth ages 12 to 18, which he hopes will activate and facilitate their faith.

Introduction

We know that all things work for good for those
who love God.

Rom 8:28

I sometimes get asked, "Why are you so intense?" Why do I yell? Why do the veins pop out of my neck? Why do I pray so fervently for the youth of America? It is quite simple. I have a son and a daughter. I have had numerous kids share with me. They tell me about the dilemmas they face growing up in our chaotic society. These kids face divorce, suicide, cutting, rape, anger, violence, prejudice, and depression. They are facing this pain every day, and someone needs to take an intense stand in defense of them. We all know that these problems are out there, but someone needs to make them *real*. This isn't Jerry Springer or the *Geraldo* show. I'm a minister.

When I was speaking at a Christian conference in Vermont a few years ago, I asked anyone to come up to the stage if in the past month, they had seriously thought about suicide. I was stunned when about twenty adults and youth came up. I started to cry. I asked them, "What caused your thoughts of suicide?"

Some said the cause was their mother; others said their father, their sisters, or their friends caused their anxiety. When I spoke at similar events in New Jersey and Pennsylvania, I heard other youth say the same thing: "My family is causing the pain, and the people closest to me are hurting me."

I doubt that the families and friends of these young people knew how much pain they were feeling. The young people of our country are speaking out, telling us what they are going through. We need to listen to what our children are saying, and we must take them seriously. Clearly we need to help America's troubled youth. How do I get these messages to families across the country?

When my wife became pregnant, my perspective changed. It made the issue even more personal. How could I allow my children to grow up in a world in which there are so many kids who have been molested, raped, who are having sex before marriage, who are addicted to drugs, who are cutting themselves, who want to kill themselves, and who are dealing with intense self-hatred and hatred toward those who have hurt them? What can we do to give our children hope? How could I keep my own children from harm?

I don't want my children to feel this hatred and pain. I don't want any children to experience it. But what could I do? I thought long and hard. I prayed. I talked with others. During a prayer God said to me in my heart, "Write a book."

I am writing this book for parents, grandparents, siblings, adults who take care of youth, and for our youth. Please, I beg you, take this book seriously. I am writing this book entreating you to help our youth. My hope is that this book will help parents and young people build positive relationships. That it will help change our interactions with young people.

We need to challenge this world full of pain and make known that there is an answer of abundant joy. One by one we can bring about change, and one by one we can make a difference in our world and bring hope back to childhood.

My hope for your children and mine is that they will find good role models who will teach them about the magnificent Love of God instead of bringing them despair, the pain of depression, and the lack of hope felt by those who are corrupting our United States.

I have been hurt at the core of my heart. I have been told that America's children cannot change; that they are problems. Some are saying that our youth are not doing anything for our culture but hurting it.

In response I say what I learned from a wise man: "If you are a leader, you are only as strong as the generation behind you." Our youth are our future, and the adults who train them need to change. Adults are the reason so many children experience such devastating problems.

Our youth are suffering mainly because adults allow others to get away with whatever they want. Too many adults say, "If it is okay with you, then it is okay with me." They say, "That is your business, not mine."

I have news for all the adults out there: That is a bunch of garbage! Children learn by example. They are hurt when they see hateful people do whatever they want. They are hurt by watching adults allow others to do as they please, even when it is wrong. Adults need to step up and become role models. Our youth need guidance from those who know what is right and feel the love of God.

I have two children growing up in this world and I do not want them looking at me, hurt, when they are ten years old and asking me, "Daddy, why are people so mean?" I don't want to have to speak the cold, hard truth, "Well, Joseph and Catherine, that is just the way it is. People don't love each other and they don't love God." The truth is, God is love, and love is God, and if we don't love, we do not know God.

Chapter One

THE CALL

*"I will sprinkle clean water upon you to cleanse
you from all your impurities, and from all your
idols I will cleanse you. I will give you a new heart
and place a new spirit within you, taking from your
bodies your stony hearts and giving you natural
hearts."*

Ez 36:25–26

Without the word of God, you have no purpose, you
have no mission, and you have no goal," I yelled.
Some of the teens in the audience shifted in their seats. I
had Joseph, my one-year-old son, in my left arm, and as he
reached out his hands trying to grab the microphone that I
was holding, all I could think was here is my heart—I do
this for you.

"How many of you have been destructive and knew you
were wrong? How many of you were afraid? I used to be
destructive and afraid. When I was younger I didn't have

a mission, and I was afraid. I didn't have a purpose, and I didn't have a goal in my life."

I paused and looked out at the young people who had gathered here today. I have to connect with them, to let them know that I am hearing them and that we are all bringing the love of God to them. I have to connect with every person sitting in front of me; it's the only way that I can really bring the full force of the message of God's love to the group.

I shared my story with them to let them know that I came from where they are now; that with God anything is possible—look at me, look at the ministry. Connecting with these young people is the most important thing that I do.

I continued. "I remember, when I was in high school, my parents took me to a psychologist. My parents and I were sitting in front of this psychologist, and I looked over at my dad. I'll never forget his expression—I could tell he was thinking about all the pain and the harm that I was bringing into my life. All the things I was doing, getting in trouble. The psychologist said, 'Justin probably won't make it into college. He'll probably have to go to a special school.' I looked to my right, where my dad was sitting, and my dad was crying."

It's hard for me to tell this story, to remember that look in my father's eye and the pain that I brought to my parents. My voice cracked as I continued the story, and I could feel myself tearing up.

"My dad was crying. Tears were streaming down his face. My dad! A guy who never cries. Because of my destructive personality! I hurt my family. I hurt my school. I hurt my friends. And I hurt myself. I did all of this because I didn't have a mission. I didn't have a purpose. And you wonder why I'm so intense, huh? HUH?" I paused to take in their breathless response. "I'm intense because I know what 'I can't' feels like. When I fail, I feel like a loser—a nothing."

That's only the beginning of the story of my conversion. The problems didn't stop there! It was much, much deeper than that. I remember getting caught by the cops for stealing a gumball machine. My father told the cop to arrest me; the cop could only laugh at me while he was reprimanding me. He couldn't believe I stole something so meaningless. Yes, one of those huge gumball machines you see in the grocery store. The one that every kid wishes they had in their bedroom. I picked it up, with three of my friends, put in my red Jeep Wrangler with the ragtop down. We took it to my friend's house.

Two days later my father got a call at his office: "Mr. Jack Fatica, did you steal a gumball machine from our store?" (At the time my father was president and owner of his own company. Why would he steal a gumball machine?) Even though I had done it, they called my dad because his name was on the insurance card for the Jeep Wrangler that we had used to steal the gumball machine! My dad laughed and told them that he certainly hadn't taken it but that he probably knew who had.

I was so bored with my life. My mission was, well, I had no mission, so I had to steal stupid things to make my life exciting, worth getting up for each day. I was told I would get caught, but I didn't care. Creating chaos was for my enjoyment, the way that I dealt with the boredom and lack of direction.

I was this caring grandson who loved his grandmothers and spent hours with them, but I was also this crazy teenager throwing boulders off of bridges onto cars, shooting cars with potato guns, lighting creeks on fire, stealing things, and so forth. Who knows what might have happened to me. Like many people told me, I was either going to make a big difference in this world or ruin the world.

My junior year of high school, I hated this priest. He was so annoying. I couldn't stand the guy, like some people can't stand me today. I'll never forget it, that day I finally drove Father Larry too far. He had just rolled into the classroom; he was six feet tall and he was a big guy. He taught at our all-boys school, and he looked tough. He wanted to let us know that he could handle us. Walking to the blackboard, he turned his back on us and began to write.

This was the opening that I had been waiting for. I smiled at my friends, took off my shoes, and threw them to the ground like I was in charge or something. Sitting in the front row, I leaned back in my chair and put my feet up on the priest's desk. I cupped my hands behind my head and smiled.

Father Larry stopped writing and turned around to face the classroom. He said, "I'm sorry that I was late for class. I got caught up . . ." He stopped talking when he saw my feet on top of the desk. Father Larry's hands dropped to his sides and he snapped, "Justin, get your feet off that desk NOW!"

"Father," I replied, "say please."

I just smirked at him. He stood silently for a moment. Then he blinked. He stared at my feet and blinked again. Now he was very angry, actually red with anger.

Father Larry's thick eyebrows met above his nose, creating a unibrow. The unibrow furrowed in rage. He rushed at my desk, knocking my feet to the floor, grabbed me by the shirt, and ushered me out into the hall. He slammed the classroom door behind us.

He backed me up against a wall and invaded my personal space. With our heads so close I could see the pores in the skin of his face and hear his rapid breathing. Father Larry really towered over me, his face painted red with rage. Spit flew from his lips as he bellowed into my face, "Get OUT of my classroom!"

The priest's voice turned stern and low. "Don't come back into my classroom until you realize your potential!" I could hear the boys in his classroom laughing and talking. They loved what was going on, but they thought I was kind of an idiot.

Father Larry's face was full of anger and resentment. "You drive me NUTS, Fatica!" he hissed. "Do not come back to my classroom until you realize your potential! Go to the office. NOW!"

After Father Larry kicked me out of his classroom, I was pissed off. As I was going down the stairwell I was swearing. "I hate that a-hole. I can't stand that guy. He drives me CRAZY!" But what I didn't know, you see, was that Father Larry cared about me. He really cared about me.

In December of that year I got a letter from him. It was a Christmas card. And I'll tell you what, I drove this guy nuts. I drove this guy to the point where his unibrow was practically falling off. You know what I mean? In the letter he wrote: "Justin, I know that I struggle with you. But that's why I pray for you every day. Because I see your potential. I see your gift. I see you as a person who is amazing and great."

At this point in telling my story to the kids at one of our events, I paused and I looked out at the group of young people watching me intently, waiting for the story to continue.

I called out to them, "And you wonder why I'm so intense, huh? You wonder why I care so much! I care because it is so important! YOU are SO IMPORTANT!"

My life was still pretty soft when I got Father Larry's Christmas card. I was screwed up, but I thought I was okay, that it was under control. I read Father Larry's words, and I thought, "Screw it. I don't care what Father Larry says. I'm going to do whatever I want. It's my life."

I used to get myself into a lot of trouble, but up to my junior year in high school, my life wasn't terrible. It didn't get scary all at once, but gradually I became more and more out of control, and eventually my life reached a horrible crescendo. Life started off soft, but bad things started to happen because I didn't have any meaning in my life. Little by little, life got louder. When I began to doubt myself and my purpose, when I lost track of the differences between good and bad—that's when my head filled with loud, lousy thoughts that attacked me from all sides. As the volume increased, I got scared. The volume in my life finally got to a level that was deafening and terrifying.

Not too long after Christmas I had a party at my parents' house while they were away. I hung out with my friends in the kitchen and in the hot tub. Some girls came over and things got pretty wild. One particular girl paid a lot of special attention to me, so I got into the hot tub with her. I took her up to my parents' bedroom and, for the first time in my life, I really messed up.

I gave myself to her. My whole heart, even though I thought it was just something teenagers did for fun. I only knew that girl one day. I'll never forget it. I told the girl that what I had done was wrong, that I was so sorry. I left her in

my parents' bedroom; I was disgusted with myself and went
to my bedroom. That night, after it was all over, I sat on my
bed hugging my wrestling buddies Hulk Hogan and Ultimate
Warrior feeling like they were my only friends. I dropped to
my knees, and I only knew two prayers. I only knew the Our
Father and the Hail Mary because I went to Catholic school.
That's all I knew, because I had never prayed much in my
life. But I prayed the Our Father and then the Hail Mary,
and I didn't stop for about twenty minutes. I was crying like
a baby. I didn't have a mission. I didn't have a purpose. I
didn't know where I was going. I didn't know what I was
doing. Something was terribly wrong. I could feel it inside,
in my heart. I cried. "Our Father, Who art in heaven . . . Hail
Mary, full of . . ." that's all I knew, and I'm crying, right?

I went to school on Monday but I was still really upset.
I must have looked it. Father Larry saw me and asked me
to go on this religious retreat called Teens Encounter Christ
(TEC). At first I said, "I know God. I don't need that. I know
God. I'm fine." Two weeks later, I told him, "Okay, I'll go."
Here's why. . . .

I hadn't spoken to the girl to whom I had given myself.
Two weeks after the party one of her friends called me to
tell me that the girl was pregnant. After I hung up I just sat
in my room not knowing what to do. I sat in my room feeling ashamed, discouraged, worthless. I couldn't believe one
time, one sin, one mistake against God could ruin my life.
The thoughts in my head were terrifying, painfully loud and
intense. My destructive life had built to this loud, terrible
crescendo.

I went to the religious retreat, a weekend-long event held
at a Catholic elementary school. I hoped it wasn't going to

be corny or something. On the first day of the retreat we sat in a classroom and listened to talks, watched skits, and played games; there were about forty of us including Father Larry and the leaders. I thought it was pretty boring until the first night when one of the adults attending the retreat set off firecrackers. Then we had to take my friend to the hospital for stitches because we were having a handclap pushup contest and he got hurt. I said to myself, Firecrackers and the hospital: it might not be that boring after all.

The next day was the start of a new life for me. Father Larry shared with us a story about a man he had known. This man had divorced his wife and left his family to go to Las Vegas. He then remarried, started another family, and eventually moved his new family from Las Vegas to Houston. One day when Father Larry was studying at the seminary he got a call from the man's second wife. She asked Father Larry to come visit the man because at 43 he was dying of cirrhosis of the liver and he wanted to talk to Father Larry. Father Larry knew that it was right to visit the man, so he flew to Houston. The man was so sick that Father Larry barely recognized him with all of the tubes sticking out of his arms. He was so thin and so weak that he could not speak, but he had a chalkboard next to his bed so that he could write notes to the people who visited him.

Father Larry spent two weeks visiting with him, and as he started to leave the room for the last time, the man waved for him to come back to him. Father Larry rushed back to his side and leaned in close to him. The man hugged him and wouldn't let go; Father Larry looked into the man's eyes and said, "I love you too, DAD!" After Father Larry shared this story with us, he told us that for years he had judged his dad, and that the only time he had told his dad he loved him was on his deathbed. He said he had been judgmental about his own father even though he was a seminarian who opened his heart to people every day.

After telling this story Father Larry talked about the importance of love. We should try to be like Jesus. Jesus loves us no matter what, and we should try to do the same. We should love Jesus more than anything.

I listened to the talk and felt confused. I asked myself, "What if I die?" I realized that when I die I want to be remembered for loving others, not for the pain I have brought to their lives. I didn't know if I loved everyone, or everything, or why it was worth loving. But I found out for the first time that in my heart God loved me, and that Jesus loved me. Could that be enough? I felt confused, empty, and lost. I thought that the least I could do would be to be honest and go into confession and say, "I'm sorry."

I entered the room being used for confession. Father Larry greeted me at the door saying, "Are you ready?" Father Larry was gentle, caring, and encouraging. He gave me a hug.

We were alone in the room, and we sat facing each other. I cleared my throat. It was hard for me to speak. "Father, forgive me. It's been three months since my last confession."

Previously I had gone to confession only because I had to. Before that day, I had gone to confession because I went to Catholic school, not because I was sorry in my heart. And typically when I went to confession I didn't talk much. I generally answered yes or no to the priest's questions. The priest used to ask me questions like "Have you helped someone have an abortion? Have you had sex before marriage? Have you cheated?"

But when I sat down with Father Larry this time, every-thing was different. I paused for a moment and then I looked up at him. "This time, I don't want to do the questions, Fa-ther. This time I really messed up. This time I really . . . "

I started crying; I was choked with tears. "This time I messed up bad. I don't want to admit it, but I had sex. And I . . . I think I got a girl pregnant."

I was crying, sobbing now; it was hard to speak. My head was messed up with terrible thoughts, loud thoughts, re-morse, and a desire to change. I started to blubber excuses for my actions. Father Larry calmly and gently put a hand on my shoulder.

"Justin," he said with compassion, "you're forgiven. You're forgiven no matter what." I couldn't believe it! I messed up bad and just like that I was forgiven. Why was I forgiven? Because God sent His son to die for me? Why would anyone die for a selfish jerk like me?

I crumbled. I just crumbled. My whole life crumbled at that moment, and the love of God built me back up. I talked with Father Larry for a long time. I talked about hurting my parents, and about the big mistakes I was making in school. I talked about how nervous I was, how scary the world was, and how loud my world had become.

Father Larry told me, "God's going to take care of it. Don't worry."

"I'm really struggling, Father. Even you, Father, I know I broke your heart."

"So," Father Larry replied, "are you sorry?"

And I really was sorry. I nodded to Father Larry. "I've got to change. And I'm going to do it, Father. I'm going to change. I'm gonna make a difference. I'm not gonna be the guy that I was before."

Father Larry gave me the biggest hug when I left and said, "Welcome home, son!"

I have never been the same since that confession. It taught me a lot. Now when I am lost I always know that confession will bring me back home again. I hated what I had done but the experience changed my life. The worst things are sometimes the things that will strengthen us to become greater people.

After I made my confession, eventually I rejoined the other people. Later that night I went to Eucharistic Adoration. (Catholics believe that when a communion wafer and wine are consecrated at Holy Mass they become the true presence of Jesus—the body, blood, soul, and divinity of Christ. During Eucharistic Adoration a consecrated host is displayed in a monstrance that is placed on the altar for all to see. People come to adoration to be in Christ's presence, to pray and speak with Him, to commune with Him.) There was a bunch of girls crying and a couple tough guys just kneeling on the floor praying. I knelt in the center of the church with people hovering around each other. I was looking up at the cross, and I was crying like a baby. And I said to myself, "God, I'll do anything for You. You saved my life. You died for me so the least I can do is die for You. You gave your life for me, so the least that I can do is give my life for You. I don't care what others think of me. I don't care about being cool; I care about loving You. I'm going to make a difference with people for You." I was kneeling in the church, and I remember that I started screaming out loud. I screamed, "I'm gonna start caring!" And I just started yelling, "I'm sorry. I'm so sorry."

And I meant it. My life had crumbled, and God was helping me to rebuild it. God was saving my life. I did change. I found my mission, to bring His love to everyone. When I tried to contact the girl, her friends told me to stay away from her. I never talked to that girl again, and to this day I don't even remember her full name, but there was no baby. Still, the experience woke me up to find the life that I needed to live.

And now I lead my life, as much as I can, for God. At the Hard as Nails events I tell the kids that I've been through all this. And God saved me. I almost destroyed myself. He saved my life. Why am I so intense? Why do I get so excited about the message? I tell them it's because if somebody saved your life, you'd do anything for Him. You'd do everything you had in your power.

I built a relationship with Jesus Christ, and I knew in my heart that He loved me. Before that experience I didn't know how much Christ loved me. I didn't know how amazing His love is. All I knew was my own selfishness. Then I got this mission, and you know what happened? I started loving my life.

The first Bible verse that I memorized was Ezekiel 36:26, and for good reason: "I will give you a new heart and place a new spirit within you, taking from your bodies your stony hearts and giving you natural hearts." Like my dad says, "He went to this retreat on Friday a jerk, didn't live his faith, had bad grades and more, and he came home on Sunday changed for life; not perfect, but with a different passion."

I became a new man and not just in my heart; I knew I

wanted to live my faith in Christ authentically. I went back to the Cathedral Preparatory School for Boys a new man with a new mission: How can I bring many people to the love of Jesus Christ? What a gift . . . what a life . . . what a passion, I thought to myself. I truly felt like the luckiest guy on earth.

One of my teachers said to me, "I don't buy this bull-s——, Fatica. You are doing this religious s—— so that you can graduate without getting thrown out."

I remember thinking to myself, He can think what he wants, judge me to the core of my soul, but I need to be like Jesus on a mission and love no matter what!

My grades the last semester of my senior year were the first miracle. I got all As and Bs. It was the first time that had ever happened in my life. I started going to daily Mass at my school, dragging as many others as I could with me, sometimes five, sometimes fifteen. I have been going to Mass at least two or three times a week, sometimes every day, since then. I got involved with a program called Heart and Soul, which was a ministry for the youth of the Catholic Diocese of Erie, Pennsylvania. It was a group run by Greg Schlueter, who was the director of youth ministry for the diocese at the time. Greg spent hours with me teaching me how to pray and how to love Christ with all my heart and soul. Greg and a team of teenagers would get in a van and travel across the Diocese of Erie, which is half the size of the state of Pennsylvania, to bring the message of Jesus to young people who attended Catholic churches. Greg taught me to be intense and authentic. He would say, "That is the way to live for Jesus," and I believed him because it worked. This was the start of my ministry as a seventeen-year-old punk.

As part of my new life I started praying in silence for

thirty minutes to an hour every day. During lunchtime I went to the cathedral next to the high school to pray. People would ask, "Where's Fatica?" "He's probably praying," would be the response.

At my graduation from Cathedral Prep I received an award for being the most influential student in the senior class. I was honored, and I believed that God wanted me to be a positive influence in the world. I wanted to please and serve Him; I just didn't know what I was going to do.

A classmate, Corey Ferraro, gave a speech at graduation and he said, "In all our lives we will never meet another Justin Fatica." I thought to myself that I needed to make a difference in this world. I truly believed that if Jesus could walk on water, maybe I, a nobody from Erie, Pennsylvania, could do something magnificent for the Lord. I didn't know what, but I wanted everyone to know the love of Jesus.

I got into a Big East Conference university. Since I loved basketball, I didn't care which Big East school I got into; I just wanted to get into one. I got rejected from the school I wanted to go to, but I knew God had a bigger plan. The bishop of Erie wrote me a recommendation for the work I had done with the diocese. The mayor of Erie wrote one for me as well; she knew me because I was a local pop (soda) vendor at the AA baseball games. She was a fan! I believe that the mayor and the bishop got me into Seton Hall University, but I also believe that God wanted me there. How else can you explain the fact that I got into this school with 820 on my SATs, around a 2.0 GPA, and a problem with ADHD?

My freshman year in college I got a 3.95 GPA, which in my book is a 4.0! God gave me the determination to work hard, and I got all *A*s! Another miracle: I have dated only one girl since I was seventeen; I didn't have sex again until I was married. Since I had messed up once already, I wanted to make sure that I followed the right path, to honor my future wife.

I truly love my life. My life is great and that is because I used to love life for me but I changed and now I love life for God. WOW! What a difference a relationship with Jesus Christ made for me! I couldn't believe it! I got into college, all *A*s; had a girlfriend who was purehearted; had a new life, a new mission, and a hope to make a big difference for Jesus Christ.

I understand how loud life can become. I want young people to know that they're not alone; so many people struggle and face pain. Together we can make it through anything. I am here to help: all of the kids and adults in my ministry are there to help, and God will always help.

God loves you. No matter what! You look at the mountain and say, "NO WAY." You look at the challenge and say, "NO WAY." God says, "You can do it. I will carry you along the way."

I learned that I could disappoint my family, I could lose all my friends, and all of my money could be taken from me, but that no one can take away my faith. No one can ever touch my faith. It is the one gift I have and will always have. Faith I cherish, faith I admire, and faith is the realization of what is hoped for. Ever since that religious retreat, my faith in Christ has been my life.

I'm Justin Fatica and I'm glad I'm alive. I'm glad I've had pain, and I have rejoiced through my sufferings. Today is your day! Make a change. If I can do it anyone can!

Chapter Two

THE MISSION

No, in all these things we conquer overwhelmingly
through him who loved us. For I am convinced
that neither death, nor life, nor angels, nor
principalities, nor present things, nor future things,
nor powers, nor height, nor depth, nor any other
creature will be able to separate us from the love
of God in Christ Jesus our Lord.

Rom 8:37–39

Once I knew that my mission was to work with young people through prayer and God's love, there was no stopping me. I talked to anyone and everyone about prayer and their faith, about the mission that I had to help people find Him, and about how Jesus would heal their pain.

My first day at Seton Hall University I decided to just start talking to people because I knew that if I talked about Christ they would follow. Anyone who thought that I was weird and different and didn't want to chill with me, I knew that they would not be my real friend anyway. I noticed right away that people were skeptical of my faith and wanted to see if it was real. Some of the students would ask me questions. I knocked on people's dorm room doors and asked them deep questions about their spiritual life. I didn't care what their answer was, whether they agreed with me or not; I just wanted them to be passionate about what they believed in. I hoped they would take a stand and believe in who they were and what they lived for. If they played sports I would say to them, "Believe in your sport first and spend all your time playing softball, and I hope it will grant you eternal life." I was intense, but I knew that I was being who God called me to be. Some of them, like Mary Zimmerman (my future wife), threw me out of their rooms the first time I met them, and others would ask me twenty questions. Either way I kept coming back and always loved them no matter what. I had fun being me, and they were entertained by meeting someone like me.

During my first week at Seton Hall University I met the president, Monsignor Sheeran, who asked me why I had come to Seton Hall. I told him, "Well, first of all, it's a Big East school and I love basketball. But most important, I am Catholic and I love the Eucharist, and here I can go to confession anytime because there are tons of priests here" (actually there were over fifty priests who worked or lived on campus). I guess that I impressed him because after that talk Monsignor Sheeran always had my back, even when it wasn't so easy to do that. He stuck up for me and gave me the benefit of the doubt. He knew I was young and immature in my faith, but he was always proud of me for my zeal. (He actually called me about the Hard as Nails Ministries documentary before it premiered at the Tribeca Film Festival. He told me that Seton Hall was very proud of the man that I am.) He always made me feel like I belonged even though I was different from the other students.

In my junior year at Seton Hall I had the opportunity to speak at a youth conference with New York Giants football players Tiki Barber, Joe Jurevicius, and so forth, but there was a Seton Hall basketball game the next day. The monsignor wanted me to be at the game to cheer on our team so he flew me from Newark to Syracuse and put me up in a hotel. He believed in my gifts, and I respected him so much for that.

Back on campus I was talking to more and more students about their faith and purpose. Gradually, two people turned into ten people and we started meeting regularly. We called ourselves the 12 Apostles; our group just kept growing larger and larger and making a real impact on the students who were involved. Everyone on campus knew who we were, and we wanted to let them know that Jesus was real and loved them no matter what!

It was during this time that I met Brian Greenfield. He lived on the same floor as the other freshmen. On the day that I met him he told me that he was going to fight an Italian fraternity because they had jumped one of his boys from the African American fraternity. I said to him, "Really you ain't jumpin' nobody." Brian had a do-rag on, he was tall, really, you couldn't miss him. I told him to come join me for prayer in St. Joseph's Chapel instead; our group, the 12 Apostles, met every week now. He told me that he would come later. I knew better. Sometimes because of my intensity people would say, "Okay, okay, I will come," but what they really meant was, NO WAY, YOU'RE TOO MUCH!

I went to the chapel to start the prayer meeting, but instead I had my friend Kerry start it and I went back to Brian's room. I told him, "I thought you were comin'." I'm glad that I went back for him because he came with me to the chapel. He didn't miss a prayer meeting the entire time that we were at Seton Hall, and he never did join in the fight with the Italian fraternity. He became one of my best friends, and today he works alongside me in the Hard as Nails Ministries. I was a groomsman in his wedding, and he was in mine. We have a bond for a lifetime.

As the size of the 12 Apostles meetings grew, I was amazed that so many people wanted to gather to talk about their faith and prayer life. We witnessed our faith within the group and did our best to stand up for what was right, for instance, by trying to keep partying under control, discouraging underage drinking or getting drunk and out of control, respecting others for who they were not what they looked like. With time, the size of the 12 Apostles meetings became an issue; we were too large to exist outside of the university administration. And eventually the university took over the group and decided to remove me from my duties as leader. They said that I wasn't ready to lead the group. They told me that I spoke with my heart first but did not have the knowledge or experience. I had to let it go and move on, so I left the group. I knew that it would be OK because my ministry was just beginning; there was so much more to do. It was meant to be.

I understood that I needed more knowledge, so I decided to read my Bible for help and guidance, and I listened to others to find out what they wanted to know about the Catholic faith. My gift was that I listened to their hearts and I shared what I knew in my own heart. I do not have a theology degree; I have a philosophy degree that helps me to understand the beliefs of others and why they believe them.

Shortly after leaving the ministry of the 12 Apostles, I was given the chance to become the assistant to the campus minister at Queen of Peace High School in North Arlington, New Jersey. I couldn't believe that at the age of twenty I was going to get paid for what I loved to do. Brother Stephen Olert, a LaSalle brother and the principal of Queen of Peace High School, believed in what I was doing. He wanted me to work with the kids on a regular basis, and I did so until he retired eight months later. The nun who took over for him did not appreciate my gifts, so I decided to leave that job.

About the same time I got evicted from my apartment. I lived in my car for a few weeks; I knew that I really needed to find a better-paying job. My father had been giving me money to live on, but I had started using my extra money to pay for friends' rent when they did not have it. Since I used my money for them and had nothing left to pay for my needs, my father finally told me to figure it out for myself. He was right; I should have been much more responsible. I kept looking for jobs I loved instead of work that would irritate me or that I didn't believe in. My mother and father always taught me to do something I was passionate about, and I knew that they were right.

In early 2000 James P. Vail at Paramus Catholic High School in Paramus, New Jersey, hired me to work as a part-time assistant to the campus minister. I helped the ministry in any way I could; I assisted with their weekend retreat program, and we started a Wednesday night meeting for the young people. He ran an amazing program, and I learned so much from him. At five he had become blind. Sometimes I would think, I need to be more like him and walk by faith not by sight (2 Cor 5:7). I was his apprentice, eagerly learning as much as I could as I worked alongside him. We had started Wednesday Night Prayer with just four young people, but I told them that first night that someday we would fill the main chapel that holds over three hundred young people. Gradually over the years that did happen.

When he was transferred from our school to a church, I got his job. I would work alongside two other campus ministers, a deacon and another layman. After I graduated from Seton Hall University in 2001, I not only took over his job as retreat coordinator and organizer of the Wednesday Night Prayer program; I also became a full-time ninth-grade religion teacher. WOW! I couldn't believe it. I was excited about making a difference. I started my master's in education at Seton Hall University and was free to build the program at Paramus as best I could.

We worked hard to make the Wednesday Night Prayer meetings events for the kids. We would play music on a CD player, with the words projected on a screen, and there would be a message about the love of Christ. I took a lot of my ideas from Protestant churches; I respected what they did because it worked. We would have Adoration and Mass some Wednesday nights, and confession too. Then something special began to happen: hundreds of young people started to come, and at school they started to pray out loud in the hallways with their friends, pray before meals in the lunchroom, go to Mass during their free periods. They committed to not having sex until marriage and to respecting all authority. Many came and a few committed, as happens in most groups, but God did amazing things at Paramus Catholic High School.

Nothing could stop us now! One of the young men from the group, Jeff Galletly, decided to start a chapter of a national ministry, Fellowship of Christian Athletes (FCA) with me. He became a leader within the ministry and on his football team. He went to college and played for Colgate University. He started for four years as a defensive lineman and played in the Division I-AA National Championship game his sophomore year. He got very involved with his faith on campus. It was then that I realized that my work at Paramus Catholic was genuine because youth were living for Christ not just when they were around me; they were also choosing to do it on their own.

Tim Hanley, a very close friend of Jeff's from Paramus Catholic who played football at Cornell University, stopped playing in his sophomore year because he believed he was called to start a ministry at Cornell. He founded the Souldiers College Ministry, which was similar to 12 Apostles at Seton Hall; it became a part of Hard as Nails Ministries. The ministry is still going strong today. Jeff also started a Souldiers College Ministry at Colgate. In Jeff and Tim, two prestigious universities had not only great leaders in athletics and academics, but also two spiritual visionaries right on campus. Jeff graduated and now works as a business consultant. He is also committed to Hard as Nails as a board member.

Tim decided to go into the Community of Franciscan Friars of the Renewal, which was founded by Father Benedict Groeschel, an outstanding priest. He joined because he believed God was calling him to serve the poor and young people, and maybe to become a priest in the near future. Not all things work out the way we plan. Recently Tim, after much prayer and spiritual reflection, realized that he was not called to become one of the friars. He now works full-time as a Hard as Nails minister. Without great leaders like Tim taking this ministry to the next level we will not flourish. His considerable gifts bring so much to our ministry.

Both Tim and Jeff were living their faith radically for Jesus Christ, and both had developed their faith through the program at Paramus Catholic High School. After college they were making a difference in very different ways, one as a leader in the Hard as Nails Ministries and the other as a successful businessman.

It became increasingly difficult for me to run the ministry and to teach at the same time; I started getting into trouble with the school administration because I used my classroom as a preaching forum every day. I had music, prayer, and a maximum of five minutes of teaching on catechesis going every day. To me, note taking and reading the book were just as important as infusing the message through sharing personal experiences, listening to music, and being entertained. My theory was that if you inspire your students they will want to learn more about religion on their own. My classroom was great and so active. Young people who had free periods would come to my class to see what was going to happen next. Being unconventional had it's downside too; I would be called down to the office at least once a week for whatever. I did not understand why something that was so positive for the kids would be such a struggle for the school administration; my students were learning so much about God's love and prayer.

Sometimes the office would receive a message from a

parent because I was just too emotional or intense about my faith in Christ. The parents would call and complain about what I was doing. They did not understand how important this was to the kids; they just didn't.

They would tell me that I needed to stop preachin' and start teachin'. They were right, but my teaching involved a lot of preaching. I realized that it was time to make a change; I had to get out of there and become a traveling preacher. But Catholics don't do that stuff. How would I make a living?

By 2002 churches had started paying me for doing talks for their students. The talks were powerful. God was doing something big, and others were beginning to see that my calling was important, that the way I delivered the message was going to make a difference. People started investing their time and money in what I was doing. They knew God had given me a gift to connect with people, especially young people, and they wanted to help.

My dad was a business guy, he owns his own company, and he told me that I couldn't be taking donations without becoming an organization. I trademarked the name Hard as Nails for the ministry; it was really different. Kids want to be part of something that isn't CHRISTIANITY IN YOUR FACE, they want something that they can relate to. I knew that the name needed to be rooted in the Bible, so I picked Romans 5:8 to explain the meaning of "Hard as Nails": "But God proves his love for us in that while we were still sinners, Christ died for us." I was confident that the hardest thing to do in your life was to love those who had sinned against you. It was easy to hurt someone but a challenge to love them no matter what! So we became the Hard as Nails Ministries.

In 2004 the ministry became a nonprofit corporation with

a board of directors; our first board meeting was in April of that year. We incorporated and received our tax-exempt status as well.

We were moving. We were on our way. We held eight Paramus Catholic retreats per year; we had the 12 Apostles program for high school students and FCA; we went to Seton Hall games and had a lot of fun. Every Wednesday night we had a program at Paramus Catholic; quietly the ministry was building. Word started to spread that this wild teacher Justin Fatica had started his own ministry for the kids, but it was taboo for the teachers and administration at Paramus Catholic to talk about it.

In January of 2005 one of my faithful benefactors gave me a Ford E350 twelve-passenger van and a trailer for the ministry with the Hard as Nails boxing gloves and cross on it. The young people couldn't believe it, the teachers were amazed, and I was astonished that little by little God was making the dream come true.

We started offering Hard as Nails events after school at churches and schools, we would practice skits in my classrooms and get ready for events at Paramus Catholic, and I got the parents to help with mailings after school. The parents were chaperones, and the people at Paramus Catholic honestly helped build the base of Hard as Nails. I would travel to Missouri or Florida to do events and have to miss school. Mr. Vail, the president of Paramus Catholic High School, would sit me down, tell me that I was double- and triple-dipping. He would laugh and say, "I thought I was a real businessman, but you blow me away."

I didn't truly understand what he meant, but more and more people kept saying this to me so I prayed about what to do. As exciting as the Hard as Nails Ministries was, it became more and more difficult to do this work out of a school. I would receive memos telling me to get the Hard as Nails van off campus before it was towed, that I needed to pay for using the school's fax machine. I knew that it was time to leave, but I didn't know how I was going to make it without a full-time job. Hard as Nails couldn't pay the bills, and I wondered who would hire me. I am too intense, and it is so hard to start all over after people have gotten used to my unconventional, unique, and intense style.

In the summer of 2003 I got married to Mary Elizabeth Fatica, the woman who had thrown me out of her room the first time I met her at Seton Hall. I love my wife not because of what she does for me, but for who we are as TEAM FATICA. We are a team, and my goal when I married her was that Mary would be my compass. If there was something that was dangerous or not the best thing for me to do, I would follow her wisdom if she felt it was not a good idea and didn't approve. That is my wife's greatest gift, her wisdom and purity of heart and mind. You see, she is my lighthouse in a dark world. When I am lost I go to her and ask her for guidance. She gives me peace and the understanding that I am loved, and no matter what happens in my life, good or bad, we have each other.

Since I had won her heart I wasn't going to let her down. I needed to be able to earn money for our future family, but at the same time I knew I couldn't run from the calling God had given me to serve Him. Mary believed in the ministry and outreach I was doing at Paramus Catholic and with the Hard as Nails Ministries. She knew that I was on the right path. She knew something was going to happen in my life.

We talked about moving to Syracuse to be closer to her family, so that she could have some support given the demands of my unique schedule. We researched living in North Jersey, and $400,000 for a house wasn't happening. I was absolutely confident, even though I was turned down for two jobs in Syracuse, that we had to move when we found out that we were expecting our first child. I had to serve my wife first.

With the move to Syracuse, I finally had to move on from Paramus Catholic, but not without first finishing the mission. The day I left the dream came true. Not all of the dreams I shared with the ninth graders came true. I had the van and I was traveling around the country talking with young people about the love of God and finding their mission in life, which shocked everyone, even me. When I left Paramus Catholic over three hundred young people showed up for my last prayer meeting. It was standing room only in Paramus Catholic's main chapel; the students gave me a picture framed from the Wednesday Night Prayer community, and it hangs in my living room to this day.

I moved to Syracuse, where these five amazing priests hired me to start Mega Youth Ministries, a Catholic youth ministry that would serve five churches in the Syracuse diocese. It has been growing strong; we now have a live band run by Bob Halligan Jr., a world-renowned musician (who wrote songs for Michael Bolton, Cher, Judas Priest, etc.). We have between a hundred and five hundred young people who come each week. It has been a tremendous community for young people and even adults. Mega Youth Ministries is making a difference and is still running.

Mega Youth Ministries is an example of what we would

like to see happen when Hard as Nails comes to a school or church. The group grows so much that they build their own ministry with a band, rappers, lights, with hundreds and then thousands of young people in one place praising God and hearing each other. Mega Youth Ministries is the example for other youth ministries of what we hope will become a niche for youth ministries all over the country and the world. Right now, Barbados, an island in the Caribbean, and New Jersey are the closest to building something like Mega Youth Ministries.

On October 12, 2005, I received the blessing that would change my life and my ministry forever. My son, Joseph Micah Fatica, was born. He had brown hair and brown eyes, olive skin, and, being biased and everything, I thought he was the most beautiful baby I had ever seen. I never dreamed of being a dad, but this was an awakening for me. I cried and cried that week, not believing that I was a daddy. I started thinking deep and real hard. My Abba, Father, Daddy in Heaven, loves me more than I could ever love Joseph. Before I became a father I was a little judgmental and not as compassionate and understanding as I am growing to be. I hurt more people than you could imagine even though I was trying to be the best minister that I could be.

The day my son was born changed me in very positive ways. He was awe-inspiring; I would tell him how proud I was of him. I thought, If I am this proud of my son, how much prouder is God of me, of everyone? I came up with this thought, thanks to my son: Atheist, agnostic, Hindu and Jew, Muslim, Catholic, Christian and even you. We are all God's children I hope you understand. It hit me hard. NO MATTER WHAT! I said it before, but I understood it like never before. NO MATTER WHAT! NO MATTER WHAT! NO MATTER WHAT, GOD LOVES ME AND YOU AND EVERYBODY. If my son gets Fs and Ds, I may be disappointed, but nothing can change the fact that I love Joseph. Nothing can change the fact that even if we are wrong, hurtful, and nasty, God loves you and me the same. WOW! My son, a little baby, touched me so much in just a few months. I thought that when I had Joseph I would sit and watch him and become less intense. I became more intense than ever before but not LOUD or IN YOUR FACE. I became more intense within my heart. I became more loving and real because of my son. My new dream was that one day my son would be able to go to school and be loved, cared for, and believed in no matter what school he attends.

My ministry changed too. The spectacle and my intensity wasn't the most important thing to me anymore. My son became a driving force so intense that when I wanted to give up I would think of him. I was crying more, laughing more, and realizing more that my son was going to live in a world where it was normal to be raped, molested, to be an alcoholic, drug addict; a place where people could be hurtful with words, where many were bullied and not loved. When I thought about not wanting anyone to hurt my son I realized I didn't want anyone to hurt anybody no matter what religion, no matter what they believed—who cares. It became more about LOVE!

One night my wife and I went out to eat and at dinner we talked about life as we often do when we are together. At the time my life was very intense. One of the youth I was working with had committed suicide and I was helping hundreds of young people and adults to cope with it. At the same time, three girls had shared with me that they had been raped; two young boys had told me that their fathers had left them. And I was meditating on the fact that that past summer at Soulfest a young man had put a knife to my throat with two hundred people watching. To top it all, a few adults and young people had threatened to kill my wife and son. I was stressed and I felt like giving up.

My wife looked me in the eyes as I was crying and she said something that I will never forget: "Justin, you can't give up." I asked her why and she told me, "Because you know why you do what you do and who is counting on you." She said to me with her whole heart, "You can't give up for him." She was pointing to my little boy, Joseph, who was sitting in his high chair twirling spaghetti.

I started to cry like a baby. "You're right, Mary," I told her. "I can't give up, and we can't give up no matter how much it hurts." It hit me hard. My son was counting on me. There are many sons and daughters in the world counting on all of us. It doesn't matter who they are or where they come from. What matters is that they are God's children and everyone deserves and demands respect.

Hard as Nails was still the same ministry, but now the entertainment with a message was secondary. What mattered most was that I give my whole heart to protecting my son and all of the children of the world. The bell rang and like Rocky Balboa, one of my favorite fictional characters of all time, I came out into the ring loving and loving with all I had. I had a mission to give it everything I had. I might be an underdog. I might be a dreamer, but so what. I was giving my life to my wife and my son. That was what mattered, and that was what I needed to do. Hard as Nails became all about love and all about acceptance and admiration for all God's people no matter what.

A few months before my son was born in 2005, I went to Soulfest for the third year in a row. Soulfest is the largest Christian rock festival in the Northeast. The event features Christian music, and the Hard as Nails Ministries run seminars for the young people attending the festival. During one of our seminars I met this guy, David Holbrooke, who wanted to start following me around with a camera. I asked my wife what she thought, and she said, "Sure it can't hurt, but what is it for?" Honestly, I wasn't sure; I figured that he was just interested in the Ministries.

By March of 2006 David Holbrooke had filmed me and the Hard as Nails Ministries many times in Syracuse, New York, on the streets of New York City, in Connecticut, Vermont, New Jersey, at Soulfest, and at lots of other places. Finally, David asked me to meet him at one of Robert De Niro's restaurants in New York City. As we ate I noticed that Robert De Niro was sitting next to us. I felt bad for the guy. He had to wear a ski cap and sunglasses in his own restaurant.

Finally, David decided to share with me that he had shown HBO five minutes of his film footage of Hard as Nails Ministries and me, and that HBO wanted to buy it for an original feature-length documentary. I asked Dave if he was kidding me! "No," he said. I was like, "WOW, but what are they going to do with the footage?" My excitement turned to worry; I wanted to do things with my life that had integrity. I hadn't thought that this footage was going to be used for anything, but this little company called Giraffe Partners, David's film company, wanted to make it into a movie. For HBO. WAIT

A MINUTE, HBO? What's the catch? Am I the fish they are going to drown in the sea? My wife and I became very nervous.

Three months before the film premiered at the Tribeca Film Festival, my wife and I were still nervous about the film, so Dave decided to let me see the finished product. After we finished watching the documentary, Mary and I agreed that we wouldn't be able to support what they put together if it stayed the way it was with no edits. We gave Dave a list of twenty things that we wanted him to change. He acted with integrity and changed as many of the things as he could. His efforts showed his heart, and even though not everything was changed, he did his best to make the film authentic. We valued his efforts. Then in May 2007 we were off to New York City and the premiere of the documentary at the Tribeca Film Festival.

I couldn't believe that what David Holbrooke, Giraffe Partners, and HBO had put together was such a positive tribute to the ministry. WOW! I thought, God is BT (Big Time!). I thought to myself, I remember when I told those young people at Paramus Catholic High School that Hard as Nails Ministries was going to shock the world. In December 2007 the documentary premiered on HBO in their living rooms, shocking them and the world. God did it all!

I couldn't have made this up, and I couldn't have dreamt what my life would be like. God is doing something amazing, and you and I are an important part of it. It could be bad, it could be good, but the future is in God's hands. I know one thing, though, eleven years ago on February 6, 1996, when I gave my life to Jesus Christ, I was a child of God and I knew that I wanted to love God, serve Him, and care for Him. And now, so many years later, the same thing is true, and I hope I can continue to keep it that simple and true.

None of this matters really. What matters is not what I do or say but that I'm a person who's striving to make a difference in this world. I am challenging people, especially young people, to do the right thing, to love God and each other. I am a guy who makes mistakes, a guy who struggles, a guy who is, you know, just trying to make a difference. That's it, that's who I am.

Chapter Three

THE MINISTRIES

"Amen, amen, I say to you, whoever believes in me
will do the works that I do, and will do greater
ones than these, because I am going to the Father.
And whatever you ask in my name, I will do, so
that the Father may be glorified in the Son."

Jn 14:12–13

The purpose of the Hard as Nails Ministries is to pass the faith and love engendered by the Ministries on to as many people as possible by training the young people who are involved to be the leaders of the future. I believe that strong leaders should encourage their followers to become leaders. There were twelve men from different walks of life who started Jesus's mission. One was a leader who needed to be transformed. Another was a betrayer who was an integral part of Jesus's ministries despite his flaws. One was loyal even at Jesus's death. Others were afraid and went unnoticed; they are now long forgotten. There were many who came to hear Jesus preach and were curious about who He was, but to all, He was a leader.

To live for Jesus Christ we must look deep into our hearts and ask ourselves who and what matters to us. Does money matter? Does fame matter? Does relying on our own intelligence matter? Simply put, what matters most to me is faith, hope, and love. These three things are the core of the Hard as Nails Ministries and they are also at the very core of Catholic teaching. They drive our mission. Love those who don't like me, absolutely. Love those who would like to see me fail, yes, every day. We must love those who have no one, who are afraid, who have been rejected by everyone else. I need to love those who are looked upon as sinners because no matter how hard I try I will always be one of those sinners begging for God's love.

At the heart of the Ministries is the message that we preach—to love each other and to build each other up in the name of God and Jesus Christ. I have spoken at large conferences to thousands of people and I have spoken to small groups of young people. Both venues are equally important in terms of the message that the Ministries brings to them. That message is that you need to live your life with God's love in your heart and to help others do the same. That is the heart of the Hard as Nails Ministries.

To create the heart of our Ministries, we need young people who are willing to step outside of their comfort zone and get involved. There are so many different roles that they can take on within the Ministries, all of which are integral to the events and the meetings that we hold as part of our outreach efforts. In building leaders within the Ministries we strive to help them to create their own unique style by sharing their powerful life stories. We try to make sure that they know that whether they volunteer by helping with the Ministries' outreach programs or by giving their lives to the Ministries of God's love, they are important to the core of the Ministries. We hope that through the time we spend with them they will gain self-confidence and learn to accept themselves for the amazing people they are!

The experience they gain from working with the Ministries can be applied to their future work lives. One of the young people who went on to become a businessman for a Fortune 500 financial company told me that after his interview with the company they said they had noticed something different about him. He felt that he didn't have the best shot at getting the job because some of the other applicants competing for the position had gone to Ivy League schools and had high GPAs, whereas he had not gone to an Ivy League school and had graduated with a 3.0 GPA. The people who interviewed him told him that he spoke with poise and confidence, and that they were impressed that he looked them straight in the eye when he spoke. He called me after the interview and thanked me and the Ministries for giving him all the opportunities to speak and run meetings as one of our leaders. He got the job! This experience showed everyone that the Ministries are a positive factor in the future success of the young people who participate.

We believe the heart of the Ministries is caring and communicating what you feel with those you love so that you can grow and become a better person in the eyes of God. It's not just about challenges but also about keeping the lines of communication open whether they are good or bad. The heart of the Ministries is communication with God and your family and friends and developing and maintaining a positive attitude toward yourself.

Hard as Nails Events

Since I have my masters degree in education I am able to speak in many different settings: elementary and secondary schools, private schools, colleges and universities, and churches. Character education is the key to developing a solid community whether secular or Christian. There are three types of events that Hard as Nails Ministries offer:

- *I am the speaker:* I speak to the group and share my life experiences with the group.
- *Team-led event:* I bring a team to share their experiences, and I also share my life experiences.
- *Open forum event:* In this event anyone attending is invited to share their challenges with the group and to become part of the experience.

The third type of event is the most intense because it gives everyone the opportunity to share very personal and intense pain with the group. Many times schools will bring me in to help them to discover what problems they are facing in their school(s). They also try to determine what they need to address with parents so that each young person can get the help they need.

Involvement in the Ministries

At the core of how we help our young people to build leadership skills is their involvement with the Ministries' events. At these events they put together skits that illustrate the challenges they face today. They create the skits themselves on topics like finding God's love, saving sex for marriage, how to have courage, how to pray, how to have a positive attitude, and so on. Some skits are serious and some are humorous, but the most important thing is that young people participate in the events/retreats because they get more out of the activities when they are involved than they would by just observing from the sidelines.

Sometimes the young people travel with Hard as Nails so that they can share their stories with the people attending an event. They tell event goers what they were like before they met Jesus personally, who they are now, and perhaps who they want to become as adults. Anyone can tell their story in this way. At Paramus Catholic High School we had weekend retreats. Youth come to a church or a designated retreat center and spend a weekend with other young people. The young people we are training to be leaders in the Ministries put together fifteen- to twenty-minute talks on a variety of topics that we have assigned them to research and present. We give them eight to ten weeks to prepare so that they can research what to include from the Bible, from the teachings of the Catholic Church, and also stories from their lives and experiences. They put their hearts into these stories. If these talks are genuine, the young people attending the retreat will get so much more from them. These talks are powerful tools not only because they give young leaders in training an opportunity to share their experiences with people who will learn from them, but also because the hours they spend preparing them is training for what they will face in a job or in life when they have to complete a task.

Awakening Spirituality

At this point, you may be asking yourself, "But how do Justin Fatica and the Hard as Nails Ministries awaken spirituality in these young people?" "How does he get their attention when they are constantly bombarded by television, movies, music, MTV, Facebook, and so much more that's going on out there to grab their attention?" We have developed several activities as part of the Ministries to help young people to understand the power of the spiritual life and to create a community among the members of the Hard as Nails Ministries.

To give you a better idea of what takes place at a Hard as Nails event or retreat, I will describe some of the most important experiences that we create at our events and retreats with our young people.

Cross Walk

The most powerful and intense experience we offer young people is the Cross Walk, which is based on the five Sorrowful Mysteries of the Rosary. To get their attention we call it the "Six Flags Crucifixion Adventure Ride." They love it because an adventure is nerve-racking. What will happen to you when you go on a roller coaster? Are you going to survive the ride? This activity is entertainment with a message.

I explain to them that I will play a Roman soldier in this adventure and they will be Jesus. With gospel rap playing in the background, we blindfold the participants so that they can focus on experiencing the death of Jesus Christ, without any distractions. This experience gives them the chance to understand the death of Jesus Christ in a whole new and very personal way. As we begin the adventure, I become silent and then shock them by shouting, "Jesus you are going to DIE."

And then we begin our journey through the five Sorrowful Mysteries:

- The agony in the garden
- The scourging at the pillar
- The crowning with thorns
- Carrying the cross
- The crucifixion

During the agony in the garden, they go into a room where very chilling music is playing, and someone circles them saying, "Jesus you are alone. All your friends fell asleep on you. Did you ever feel like you had no friends? Did you ever feel like ending your life because of this? Jesus, you are going to die soon. You are so scared, Jesus, that you are sweating blood. Do you want to go through with this? Do you want to be courageous? Do you want to die for people who won't even care?" We ask them so many questions because Jesus was asking himself a lot of questions as he meditated in the garden of Gethsemane. The message that we want them to understand from their experience of the first Sorrowful Mystery is that Christ was fully human.

The second mystery, the scourging at the pillar, re-creates the whipping that Jesus was given as He stood up for us. As explained in Isaiah 53:5, "He was pierced for our offenses, crushed for our sins, Upon him was the chastisement that makes us whole, by his stripes we were healed." While each young person is leaning against the wall, we hit the wall next to them with a belt and scream, "Jesus, you took the pain and suffering for those who picked on people, who worried about how they looked instead of how they treated people, who have had sex before marriage, who have gossiped." We scream up to thirty different sins so that they get the point that He was pierced for our transgressions.

In the third mystery Jesus is crowned with the crown of thorns. This reenactment lasts for only about ten seconds and is done on the way to the hill where they will carry the cross. We place our crown of thorns, a woven crown of sticks, on their heads and then we gently wipe Q-tips down their face to mimic the feel of sweat and blood dripping down Jesus's face. This helps them to understand that He felt not only the agony of losing His friends and being ridiculed and destroyed by whips, but also the mockery and the pain of wearing the crown of thorns: "Weaving a crown out of thorns, they placed it on his head, and a reed in his right hand. And kneeling before him, they mocked him, saying, 'Hail, King of the Jews!' " (Mt 27:29).

In the fourth mystery Jesus carries the cross. As the person playing Jesus carries the cross up the hill, leaders are screaming Bible quotations at them, yelling, mocking, and ridiculing them. One of our adult chaperones helps the blindfolded person up the hill like Simon of Cyrene did for Jesus. The person carries a cross that is bigger than they are and weighs about twenty-five pounds. This experience helps them to realize how far He went to show His love for us. As they carry the cross up the hill, we shout things to them like "Are you going to give up now, Jesus? You are not cool anymore, Jesus. You are a loser because you are doing the right thing. Give up now?" This reflects the battle that we all go through by just wanting to be a good person. Jesus does not want us to strive to be good; we are already good. He wants us to be great for the world to see.

The fifth and final mystery is the crucifixion. We lay the young person on the cross that they have carried up the hill, taking large nails and laying them on their hands where Jesus was nailed. We then take a hammer and hit the cross intensely next to their hand saying, "Die, Jesus, for people who don't even care." We repeat to them, "For God so loved the world that he gave his only Son, so that everyone who believes in him might not perish but might have eternal life" (Jn 3:16).

We leave them lying on the cross on the ground for a short time while a song by David Meece plays in the background. The words to the refrain of the song are, "We are the reason that He gave his life. We are the reason that He suffered and died. To a world that was lost He gave all He could give to show us a reason to live." This song sums up what the Cross Walk is all about. Then we pick the young person up from the cross, give them a big hug, and tell them, "Jesus loves you so much."

At the end of the Cross Walk the youth leader, the priest,

and the adult leaders of the group pray for the person and listen to them. This time is powerful for them. The youth leaders know each young person individually, and during this time they pray together and listen to each other's hearts. I love this part of the retreats because it is so important for them to share with the leaders who will be with them after the Hard as Nails team leaves.

Walking the Cross

The Walking the Cross activity is different from the Cross Walk. As someone in the group carries the cross up the hill, the young people and their leaders walk alongside them up the hill at Soulfest in Gilford, New Hampshire, while they share their challenges and pain with each other—the "crosses" they have had to bear in their lives. The act is like a prayer to remember what Christ did for us and also to walk their personal "crosses" up to Jesus. It is a spiritually moving experience because the young people and leaders are sharing their deepest feelings and are praying for each other.

The Piñata

Another powerful experience at Hard as Nails events is the Piñata, which provides an opportunity for us to take our pain and expose it so that sweetness can come from it. The Piñata activity is focused on understanding the pain of the world and the horrifying experiences our young people can go through. Whether it is depression, rape, suicide, addiction, or something else, something good can come from these challenges.

A piñata is hung in the school gymnasium or in the church hall, wherever the event is taking place. First I share the pain that I have experienced, and each time I share a painful time in my life I hit the piñata with a bat. Next I ask a team leader to come up and share the pain they have experienced in their life, and they hit the piñata. I then ask the group if anyone has experienced what the team leader has experienced. If they have, I encourage them to come up and just hit the piñata or to share their own story with the group if they feel comfortable doing so.

One time a young man came up in front of three hundred young people and adults. He grabbed the bat from my hand and said, "I have never told anyone this in my life. When I was eleven years old my uncle molested me, and the next day my mother came to my room and told me that he had hung himself. I have had to deal with that pain since then." I shared how much I felt for him and asked if anyone in the group had been through a similar experience. I asked them to come up and join him. At least fifteen people came up to the piñata and gave him a hug. I believe that he was healed that day, that a huge burden was lifted from his shoulders, and that he got the courage to move on with his life. It's amazing to watch how people at these events give each other courage and the will to start over.

As more and more people in the group tell their stories, the piñata is continually hit until it weakens and then with the final whack the candy streams out onto the floor. The message of the Piñata activity is that sharing your pain can bring sweetness into your life once again. I tell them; "Remember that you can make your mess into a message."

Young People Tell the Story

Why do we do the things that we do to other people? Do we even think about how it affects them? Sometimes the only way to make this point to young people is to shock them by showing them how much it hurts to be the person who is being hurt or made fun of. At some events I bring an overweight leader with me to help the kids to understand how it feels when other people put you down. First, I talk to them about how people hurt other people all the time without thinking about it at all.

What if people really knew our secret feelings? What if they knew the truth of how jerky we can be or about the things that we have done when no one was looking? They probably would not like us! I tell them that my overweight friend has a challenge and that she gets hurt every day for it. I tell them to look at her—it's obvious to everyone what I am about to say out loud to them, that this girl is FAT! The whole place cringes and gets upset at what I have just said out loud. I tell them not to get upset with me because I am just saying out loud what all of them were thinking, reflecting how people treat each other. Her challenge is out there for everyone to see. She is FAT, and if she wasn't, more people would hang out with her. Isn't that the truth?

The young girl then shares her story of how hard it has been for her to know that while people don't say it to her, she knows that they think it. Then I go wild and start saying crazy things like "You're Chinese! Do people get judged for that?"; "YOU CUT YOURSELF! Do people get judged for that?" "You're MUSLIM! You're CATHOLIC! You're PROTESTANT! YOU HAVE A BIG HEAD! YOU ARE ON

PRESCRIPTION DRUGS! DID YOU KNOW THAT SHE WAS RAPED? DID YOU KNOW THAT HE IS REALLY DEPRESSED? YOU'RE AN ALCOHOLIC! YOU'RE A DRUG ADDICT! SHE IS A SLUT! YOU'RE A LOSER!" And on and on.

Finally, I ask how many of them can relate to this girl. "Have any of you been called a name or had people talk about you behind your back?" They all say yes. How much does it hurt? Does it make you feel like garbage or worthless? Yes, they tell me! Many of us have challenges that no one sees or understands. Why don't you hang out with fat girls, or the guy with a big head? Why don't we accept someone who is gay? Sometimes the stupidest things make us not want to hang out with one another or to care about each other. What would have happened if Jesus had done that to the people around Him? He could never have done that to any of us, and we need to follow His lead in this and not do it to each other. It is time for us to change and to accept each other the way we are. "You are the ones to begin this change!" I tell them. "NOW IS THE TIME AND YOU ARE THE ONE!"

Intensive Prayer

We pray with people constantly as part of the Ministries. We have intense healing Ministries. The first thing we do is listen to the young people, to their pain and their challenges. There are many opportunities for them to share with us. It can be at lunch, in a small group session, during the event, at the Piñata activity, after the Cross Walk, or at any time. Before the end of an event we have a closing prayer session that provides another opportunity for us to listen to their hearts and to pray with them. Listening is the most important thing that we can offer them. When others in the group see that we are listening they know we care. This helps the healing process, since they need to share their hearts and be real so that God can move through their whole body and soul.

After they share their pain with us, we have personal prayer sessions, calling them up individually so that they can pray with our team leaders. This is a powerful experience. Each gets the personal attention that they need to talk and share their pain with us, and then we pray for them by placing our hands on them and asking that God heal them. They share challenges they face with their families, and we pray for God to protect them. They tell us how deeply they have been hurt by a boyfriend or a girlfriend, and we pray that God will heal their broken and troubled heart.

The Intensive Prayer time is one of my favorite times during an event because I have personally seen God work miracles right before my eyes. Many times the young people cry, and I usually cry too, because I can feel their pain moving from their hearts to my heart to God's heart.

We have developed strong faith-based communities in Connecticut, Vermont, northern New Jersey, New York City, Saint Louis, Missouri, the annual Soulfest event in New Hampshire, Washington, DC, and Barbados. Within each community we have a community leader, adult volunteers, and youth leaders. The communities are growing constantly.

Hard as Nails is all about intense love. Love "bears all things, believes all things, hopes all things, endures all things. . . . Love never fails" (1 Cor 13:7–8). Let your love be intense because love covers our sin. This is what the Bible says, and this is what Hard as Nails stands for. When all else fails, love. Our role as ministries is to believe in others, encourage others, and to love others no matter what.

Chapter Four

THE HEART OF
THE MINISTRIES

But God proves his love for us in that while we
were still sinners Christ died for us.
Rom 5:8

When young people share deeply profound challenges
or successes, as Amy does in the story that follows,
I tell them that their message is for someone whom I could
never touch. I respond to them with my heart, with my tears,
and by listening to their needs. As part of the process we
reach out to the person who has shared their experience with
the group and ask them if they are in counseling or seeing
a psychologist. If they are not, we refer them to a volunteer
doctor who works with Mega Youth Ministries and helps
them to get the professional help and guidance they may
need to heal.

Many times after young people share their stories I ask

that those who have had similar experiences join us and give some hope to the person who is sharing so that they can get through their difficulties. We are in this together, and we are there to support them in any way that we can. There are also volunteers at each meeting watching for young people who have not shared before or who might be having a difficult time. They go up to the young person and talk to them, to see if they want to share one on one. And if they want help, they refer them to someone who can help them.

Young people share at the events weekly, and I believe that having a community committed to them is very good medicine. We have events almost every week except for holidays; even on bad weather days we show up so that the young people know how seriously dedicated we are to them (in Syracuse there are a lot of snow days). The young people know that there is always a place where they can go, and even if they have not been for a while, they know that they can come and share and be accepted.

I've been lucky in my life. I grew up in a great family and did not experience much that was negative or challenging in my life, but, as I wrote earlier, in my youth I was directionless. My brother who went to Temple University is now a very talented businessman; he's an amazing communicator and naturally smart. My sister went to Boston College and is a brilliant leader who has worked in human resources for many companies. When I was in high school I didn't have any idea who I was or what I wanted to do with my life. And the pressure to succeed in my family was intense. I figured that the best way to succeed would be to set really low expectations for myself. If I didn't commit to anything then I could do what I wanted to do or I could do nothing at all—and no one would care. Wrong! I ended up acting out and blaming my personal failings on everyone else.

When I finally found Jesus Christ I learned how to open my heart to what others were feeling, to be able to cry with them and to laugh with them. How to help them experience God's love for them. The Bible taught me to rejoice with those who are rejoicing but also to mourn with those who are mourning. Too often we are told that time will get us through our troubles, or that because someone else has been through something that we are now experiencing we should be able to cope in exactly the same way they did. I do not believe this kind of thinking has any part in the healing process. I believe that listening and emotionally connecting with the person who is suffering are the way to help others heal.

This is the greatest lesson that I have learned from Jesus. He laughed with his friends at a wedding when he probably was agonizing about the death that he would endure in a few short years. He had the right idea. Weep with those who are weeping and rejoice with those who are rejoicing. Jesus showed me that I need to take my heart and feel love and acceptance for every person I meet. Each time I lead or am part of the team leading an event, my heart is challenged by the stories that the young people share with us.

Because the young people can feel that I want to help them find their way, a lot of them, and also adults, share their stories with me, no matter how terrifying and heartbreaking they may be. They share their hearts with me and I feel their pain. We help them to take that critical first step of sharing their story with people who care about them. That is what Jesus did for us.

In the following pages we share the stories of five young

people and a young father, each story dealing with a different type of pain. By sharing their stories these people were able to open their hearts to the love and acceptance of God and the community of the Hard as Nails Ministries. I hope that as you are reading these stories you feel their pain, are able to open your heart to find a way to help people, young and old alike, who are challenged to find love in this world. They need you and they need Jesus.

I cry every day. When you get a glimpse of what I hear on a daily basis, you will understand why I am so passionate and persistent about getting young people and adults—YES even adults—to open their hearts. Just because they are reluctant to tell their stories doesn't mean that they do not need help. Come with me on a journey of understanding, where we can learn how much love we need to give to people so that they can live happy, healthy, and spiritual lives.

I hope that you will think twice when you see an angry teenager or adult; maybe they need your love. We never know what someone has been through until we love them so much that they share their hearts with us. I have learned that no matter where you go there are people who need our love and God's love. May you never forget that God made you AMAZING!

Amy's Story: Rape

Justin Speaks

I had heard the news about a fifteen-year-old girl being raped in her hospital bed, but it had seemed too "out there" to be real. Back in January 2006 I noticed a shy, quiet girl sitting in the back of one of the Mega Youth Ministries events that we hold in Syracuse, New York, every Wednesday night. I learned that her name was Amy (not her real name). I was having a training program for Mega Youth leaders that week, so I invited her, even though it was only her fourth or fifth time coming to the Mega Youth Ministries events. I really believe that if you give someone a chance, they will surprise you. And why not? Jesus gave Peter a chance without asking him any questions about who he was or what he did.

I had no idea what I was going to witness in the next few months with Amy. I really don't think about what a young person might share with the rest of us or what they might have been through. Everything and anything can come up at one of these events: suicide, rape, abuse, violence, attitude problems, family incest, or whatever. I really only care that people are coming to be part of the group and that through the love of Jesus they can be helped.

When Amy came to our event on that Sunday in January she seemed exhausted. As I do at every event, I asked all of the youth to come up and be prayed over. There was a song playing in the background called "Healing Rain" by Michael W. Smith. Amy came up with a friend and she was crying. Then she told us, with every ounce of strength she had left, "I was the girl in the newspapers and on the news who was raped in the local hospital. I didn't really know my room-mate, and her boyfriend brought a guy with him when he visited her that night. When they left the room, he grabbed me, held me to the bed, and raped me. I feel like I can never trust anyone again."

As I heard her say all this, I was astonished and heartbroken. Many times young people have told us about being raped, but never while in the hospital where they were getting help and should have been safe and protected. I couldn't believe what I was hearing. I was crying, and all I could do was hug her. And I prayed with all my heart while I was hugging her. She didn't run away; she opened up her arms. I believe that God heard our prayers, and the hug I gave her that day started the intense healing process she was going to need.

At the Mega Youth events young people usually talk in big groups; it falls to me to ask the tough questions like "How many of you have been raped?" That day when Amy shared her story, six or seven young people came over to hug her, and we surrounded her with the love and tears that I believe she had been waiting to receive for a long time. Then all the kids who were lucky enough to have never been through such a traumatic experience came up and hugged Amy.

After I experience a young person sharing such a tragedy I usually bring the meeting to a close by talking about others who have been through tough times, and I remind them that we can help each other if we go through it together. Once the event has ended I reach out to the person who has shared, as I did with Amy, to make sure they are seeing a counselor or a psychologist or are in treatment of some kind. If they are not, I refer them to a volunteer doctor who works with Mega Youth who can get them the help they may need.

We helped Amy through all the phases of her trauma, including spending the day with her when she was going to testify against her attacker in court. One of the other volunteers and I took Amy to a movie, to take her mind off what she was about to do. Amy is now moving forward with her life. She used to come to our program every week, but now that she has gained confidence she is there once or twice a month. When Amy was really hurting she needed the community every week, but now she has moved on to greater things. She wants to be a nurse or maybe even a religion teacher. She wants to heal people like she was healed. She travels across the country now with the Hard as Nails Ministries, helping other young people, and she has the gift of being able to listen to and care for those who are hurting. I believe that she has realized that her pain was her greatest gift to this world, and that sharing her story will now help many other young people.

She is doing very well in school and just got 1350 on her SATs. She attends a Catholic high school and pays her tuition by working many hours during the week. She has been a gift to the high school. Many youth have been inspired by her story and have decided to get the help they need.

Amy Speaks

1. What struggles did you have in your life?

As a child I got along with both parents fairly well, but as I got older my relationship with my dad was very strained. It was hard sitting in a room with him without fighting. That got worse after June 28, 2005. My life was changed forever that night! I was sick and had to go to the Emergency Room and then was admitted to the hospital. I stayed there for seven or eight days so they could figure out what was wrong with me. While I was there I was attacked and raped by a guy my roommate's boyfriend brought to our room one night for a visit. After he raped me he just walked away. How could that happen? Why did that happen? So many thoughts rushed through my head. What was God thinking? was also a big question. I shut off all feelings. I was SO sick and didn't have anyone to help me through it, or so I thought. I knew other rape victims were out there, but where? I was struggling alone with being raped in a hospital room by a complete stranger. I felt ugly and worthless. My main conflict was within myself, about not feeling good enough. When I finally went to a Mega Youth Ministries meeting there were all sorts of people. Everyone was so accepting and loving. It was a community filled with the support I needed to go through my everyday life while fighting my inner self. This community was just what I needed.

2. How did you first come to the Mega Youth Ministries?

Last January Ricky, a friend of mine, asked me what I was doing on Wednesday nights. I responded that I wasn't doing anything, and that was true. I was new to the school and really had no extra activities in my life. I was very lonely, so when Ricky invited me to this Mega Youth Ministries meeting, I agreed to check it out. I started going to the weekly meetings. As I walked into the church where the event was being held I felt at ease. I sat at the back of the church while many kids sat in the front of the church. I was raised Catholic, but after the rape I had stopped going to church because I had stopped believing. A few weeks after I started attending the Mega Youth meetings Justin Fatica invited me to attend a training weekend for some of the youth of the Mega Youth Ministries community. This was big for me since it would be my first night away from home in over six months, since the rape. I was very scared and didn't know why I was doing this. The girls and boys were separated into sleeping areas, so I found a place for my sleeping bag next to a girl I knew who went to my school, and as the lights went out we started talking. I was hinting at my situation, and she came right out and told me she had been raped, and my head spun! I thought, God, you sent her here for me. We talked for hours, and then the next day I stood in front of all the kids at the training meeting and told them I had been raped. All of a sudden everyone was standing around me singing, and I don't know what came over me, but I reached out to Justin Fatica and blurted out my story, poured out my soul to people I didn't even know. Right after telling them I had to run to the restroom and throw up, but I felt so free having people know. I wasn't fighting it alone anymore. I had people who knew and were going to try to understand. A few months after speaking for the first time about my rape, I spoke to my whole high school about what had happened to me. Girls came up to me crying and saying they were so sorry, and guys came up to me and hugged me. I was scared to death because people were touching me, but I still let them come and support me. And all of that support from the community helped me heal day by day, thanks to the love and support of newly made friends and the love of our Heavenly Father.

3. Did people come and talk to you about your experience?

After I was done speaking about my rape, some people came to talk to me one-on-one, and some kids came in groups just to ask questions or wish me well. I felt very empowered and felt comfortable being in my own skin again.

4. After standing up in front of your school how did you feel?

I felt like I belonged there. I was welcomed with open arms; people understood me and knew where I was coming from. With God in my heart I was able to tackle many obstacles.

5. Do you miss the program when you're not around?

When I have to be somewhere else other than Mega Youth meetings on Wednesday nights I feel like I'm missing something. MYM has become like a family to me, and without my "family" I'm just lost.

6. How did God's love bring you through this?

I think that God gave me the strength to overcome my pain. All those times I wanted to give up, God was there beside me telling me to go forward, and sending people to encourage me. Justin created a family for me at Mega Youth Ministries. Without God's constant love I would never have been able to overcome my struggles over the past year. Some days when I feel low and withdrawn I pray to God and regain my strength. In my days of triumph I also pray to God and feel comfort in knowing that He is with me.

7. Did people respond to you differently after you shared your story?

After speaking about my struggles with my family and the rape I was received with open arms. I thought I was a disgrace, but really that was all in my head, and everyone around me was supportive and helpful. Without the community I found in Mega Youth I never would have made it this far. I found out that it's not my fault that I was raped. It's not my fault that I couldn't fight back. So with God's undying love I am now fighting for new reasons! I'm fighting all the hatred in the world and just trying to take life day by day, and I'm not doing half bad.

Rocky's Story: Self-Acceptance

Justin Speaks

Rocky was seventeen years old when I met him at Bishop Ludden High School. He was a jokester, a student who didn't excel in school, a jerk to teachers and anyone who didn't fit into his group. He played basketball, football, and soccer—he was a real jock! He only hung out with kids who made him look cool; teachers dreaded having him in class because he was a goofball and just plain nasty. But he had a good home life; although his parents were divorced, they got along well. Rocky called his parents "underdogs" because they were always trying to improve their lives and those of their children.

With strong parental support at home, why did he act up in school? He was obnoxious and hurtful at school, making fun of anyone who was different, but he couldn't stop because he was afraid that he would lose his friends. Rocky would make prank calls to all of the teachers he had that he didn't like. There was one teacher, though, who finally tried to force Rocky to stop, to change his attitude.

Throughout the entire school year they went back and forth until finally one day the teacher yelled at Rocky and told him that he was "a nuisance" and that he couldn't even stand being in the same room with him. Rocky looked up at his teacher with a smile and said, "Don't worry, the feeling is mutual." Yet when the school administration had meetings about Rocky's discipline problems, the teacher would stick up for him. In class he gave Rocky a hard time about his attitude, but when the administration was on the verge of expelling Rocky from school for good, he came to his defense. Later, after Rocky came to Christ, he really thought about this and decided to apologize to all his teachers whom he had disrespected, and this teacher was the first one he approached!

As I said earlier, I had met Rocky at Bishop Ludden High School, before he ever attended a Mega Youth event; I saw a little of the old me in Rocky. One day I decided to ask Rocky to come on a Hard as Nails tour to Vermont with me and six other students. Because his grades were so low, his teachers were not in favor of his going on the trip, but I convinced the principal that if Rocky joined us, it would change his life forever.

We had the film crew from HBO traveling with us, so the trip was very interesting and exciting for the students. I had every young person share their stories the first night. Rocky told us that his brother was in jail and that his parents were divorced; that he had been a jerk to many people, and that the year before he had had sex with a girl because he felt pressured to do it. This tough guy the school authorities thought couldn't change began to cry. He was begging God for help; he wanted to change. Rocky told his story to thousands of youth that week in Vermont; he touched their lives and gradually his life began to change. I think that he was genuinely surprised at how the other kids at the retreat responded to him; it humbled him and made him share who he really was, just a kid trying to be accepted by the other kids at his school.

When Rocky got back to Syracuse his friends started calling him Rev. Rock because he was changing his life, and they were trying to get under his skin. In joining Mega Youth Ministries he discovered that he was being himself for the first time, not trying to be someone who hurt people but someone who listened to the other kids and tried to help them. He started to play soccer and to work toward improving his grades so that he could go to college. He began to change his one-on-one relationships so that they were more positive and not hurtful, especially his relationships with girls. Many of the people whom he had made fun of and been nasty to were now part of his Mega Youth community. Interestingly, by being himself Rocky has been able to maintain his old relationships as well as his new relationships. Many times I have seen youth struggle with losing old friends because of the changes they have made in their Christian lives, but this was not the case with Rocky. It was amazing to see!

His life has continued to change in amazing ways. He now goes to college and plays soccer, but he is also helping the campus ministry to develop its programs. Everyone who meets Rocky says that he is real, and that he knows who he is and what matters most to him.

A million-to-one shot changed his life. That is what happened to me; it can happen to anyone. I remember that when I was eleven years old I would come home after school and watch Sylvester Stallone's *Rocky* movies over and over again. After being thrown out of class or having lunch detention I would need a pick-me-up, and those movies inspired me.

Can Rocky (the kid) really change? They were right to ask me, but when people told me that I couldn't do something or that there was no way that I was ever going to change, my *Rocky* theme music would start playing in my head: "It's the Eye of the Tiger, it's the thrill of the fight rising up to the challenge of our rival." That's why when teachers, parents, or anyone says that a young person I am working with cannot change I really can't listen to them because I was like that and I changed. Anyone can change when they are supported by the love of God and people who are willing to listen to them.

Rocky told me that some of his friends' parents had asked him why he was with the Mega Youth Ministries; they had heard that only the kids with a lot of problems go there. He didn't understand why they would think that way because we are all facing a lot of challenges, weaknesses, fears, hurts, and pain. If everyone realized that sometimes they need help to improve their lives, it would be a better world.

God is real. God can do the impossible! I am so proud of Rocky and all of those who have changed when no one else thought they could. Today is the day to discipline your mind to the true fact that with God anything is possible. No matter how hard life gets, no matter how much it hurts, no matter how much pain we feel inside, God can help us through anything! Now is the time to be the one; change your life and make a difference.

Rocky Speaks

1. What was your home life like? Do you have brothers and sisters? Do you get along with your parents?

My parents separated when I was a baby. They shared an equal amount of time with me as I went back and forth from mom's house to dad's house. They did a great job staying civil, and they always put my upbringing ahead of their problems. My mom always believed in me even when I really struggled. She had it tough growing up. She fought for me when everybody else was giving up. I get my heart from her. My father was the disciplinary figure in my life. He was also very loving. He always told me that I was his second chance in life. Like I was some kind of hero, and all I did was be born. It always made me feel worth something. He struggled the most with my problems in school. We would fight every day when I was a sophomore/junior in high school. I would run away almost every weekend. Although he showed anger, I knew he loved and cared about me and this was just how he dealt with his worries. He started seeing counselors to help deal with me. This made me feel guilty. I felt like I was letting everybody down. I always felt bad and often cried after fighting with my dad. My sister, who is in her thirties, now lives in Pennsylvania. She is married with two children. She is beautiful and gives me hope that things can turn out well in my life. My brother, also in his thirties, has been in and out of prison for the past ten years. I always wanted him in my life. The idea of having an older brother for me was really cool. Because of his turbulent life I didn't get to spend much time with him. I've written to him on many occasions, but he rarely writes back. My brother is not a bad man or some scumbag because he is in prison. He just messed up a few times. When I think about my life, I can honestly say that I probably would have ended up in prison like him if it hadn't been for this dramatic experience I had in high school. How can I not love my brother because they say he is a criminal? I love him regardless.

2. Why did you act up in school and with others?

Why not? What's the point of being a square, like everybody thinking inside the box. Do this, do that. Do your homework. Listen to your teachers. Don't mess up. Screw that. To me that was just boring. I didn't want to be like everybody else. I wanted to be *the man*. I wanted to be noticeably different. I didn't get the point of following the rules. Were these teachers better than me? Most of their rules were just stupid anyway. Why should I follow them? So I did my own thing.

I grew up in the east part of the city, and my high school, Bishop Ludden Catholic High School, was in the west part of Syracuse. I was placed in a school where everybody had grown up together and had gone to Catholic grammar school together. They shared all these memories with each other from their childhood. The only reason I was there was because my parents put me in Catholic school after I started causing trouble in public school. My childhood didn't mean much to the other students; they didn't share in it. They had big houses and money, and almost none of their parents were divorced. I came from an apartment, and it seemed like my family had problems that their families didn't have. This was not true of all of my classmates, but many of them seemed to have no struggle. They seemed somewhat fake and idealistic to me, but I still longed for their acceptance.

I got in trouble a lot and my classmates loved that. They thought I was hilarious and entertaining. They were amused by my general "I don't give a care" attitude. I was really just being myself at first, and then I saw how much the kids liked me for it. To me it didn't matter what my teachers thought; they were just old and didn't understand. All that mattered to me was that my classmates, at least the cool ones, loved me for what I was doing. I didn't get the point of not rebelling. Was I supposed to just do as I was told and play the good kid role just because they said so? Or so I could get some nine-to-five job when I was older? Gimme a break; I was in tenth grade. If I was gonna do what they wanted me to do, I would have to give up the adoration that I was getting from the kids at school, and that mattered more to me than anything. I was driven by that respect, but I knew I wouldn't get it if I wasn't playing sports or didn't look good. All that mattered was that I had that admiration from my classmates. I would constantly mock those who were not considered cool at school. The fat girls, the nerds, the Star Trek geeks. I use to call them UFOs, and people got a kick out of that. For me, teachers were no different than students, so I mocked them and acted out against them too. Most of the teachers hated me, and the outcasts at school thought I was the biggest jerk. I got detention or was suspended nearly every day of my junior year. I almost got kicked out of school three times. I didn't care that they already thought I was a screwup, so I was going to stick it to them as best I could.

3. What first inspired you to come to the Mega Youth Ministries?

I came to Mega Youth after going on the Hard as Nails retreat. My experience on the retreat inspired me to come to Mega Youth. I knew that it was within my power to make a big change in my life.

4. How did you feel after you shared your story with other young people during the Hard as Nails tour?

I was talking to a group of total strangers. I knew it was an opportunity to share something from my heart. I got stuff off my chest that I felt nobody at home could understand. I shared my heart with people after years of hiding it. It lifted a real weight off my shoulders. Sharing my story helped me to realize who I really was and encouraged me to believe that maybe I wasn't just a jerk and that I really did care about people. I felt like I had a chance to be myself, no cover. I didn't have to act hard. I just let go. It made me feel worth something again like when my dad told me that I saved his life.

5. Did people come and talk to you about your experience? Did people respond to you differently after you shared your story?

I had no idea that people would respond. I was just trying to break these shackles I felt like I was wearing. I was just letting my heart pour out. I did it more for me than to help anyone. But people really responded. Many young girls and boys came to me and told me that they were touched by my story and were able to relate to certain parts of it. For the first time in my life I learned that the best way to help people is to reveal your weaknesses and your struggles to them. Kids shared their stories with me. Girls told me of their struggles with being raped and guys of their struggles with sex, drugs, and alcohol. It was somewhat overwhelming, but I could see in their eyes that they trusted me, and it made me feel special.

6. How did Justin help you to prepare yourself to tell your story? What has his support meant to you?

Sometimes people don't realize that doing little things in life can mean so much to other people. Justin came into my life at a time when the adults in my life had given up on me. So when Justin invited me on a retreat, though it may seem like a small thing, to me it was huge. I was desperate for someone to believe in me. I was crying in the school counselors' offices, failing in school; I was ineligible for sports and about to get kicked out of school. I felt like I had hit rock bottom. I probably would have just laughed at the thought of a religious retreat, but the fact that I got invited to something by an adult really touched me, and plus things couldn't have gotten much worse, so I said yes. The teachers said I couldn't go, but Justin really stood up for me and convinced them to let him take me. When Justin told me his story I knew I was there for a reason. I felt just like he did when he was seventeen. The similarities were almost eerie, and I related so much to what he went through at my age. When I saw the people he touched with his story, it made me feel like if I changed maybe I could make a difference, too.

7. Talk about the impact that God's love has had on your life. How did God's love bring you through this?

I'll never forget sitting in that Vermont church on the last night of the Hard as Nails retreat. I was the only one in the church. As I was sitting there in that empty pew facing the altar I couldn't take my eyes off the large wooden cross where Jesus was hanging. Before then I had never read the Bible or studied any Scripture. I wasn't even making good grades in school. But I felt God's love. It was alive in my heart. I could feel Him, and for that moment it all made sense. Everything was clear. The whole world was still crazy around me, but here, in front of Jesus, was nothing but peace. I knew what He was calling me to do. The world had it wrong. People had it wrong. They weren't focused on Jesus and loving people. And He wanted to use me—a nobody, a jerk from Syracuse, New York—to bring people to His Love. I was completely humbled. I couldn't deny Him anymore. I had hurt so many people and He loved me anyway. I knew I had to change.

Angela's Story: Sex Addict

Justin Speaks

The first time I met Angela at Mega Youth I told her that she needed to stop running and hiding from her problems; she needed to realize that she could be forgiven for her sins. After she had been to a few meetings, I asked her to get up in front of the group and tell her story. I knew that this would be tough for her, but it was an important step for her to take so that she could fully accept God's love and forgiveness and realize that she was an amazing person.

Hesitantly she told us about her home life. She had a good relationship with her mother, but not such a good one with her stepfather or her sisters. Her mother was supportive but was fighting her own addictions; her stepfather was part of the family but not really involved in her life. It was only in the past year that she had found out about the existence of her birth father. Her mother had never told her about him or that he lived so close to them. Angela was a young girl by herself trying to figure out how to live in this world with no guidance, on her own.

She told us that her mother had told her that if you love someone, having sex with them is the most important thing that you can do to show them that you love them. Desperate for love and acceptance, Angela had sex for the first time when she was ten years old. I thought to myself, Oh my goodness, ten years old. How is that possible? But sex was not her only addiction; she had also been addicted to drugs and alcohol since the age of ten!

At eleven she was already in a sexually abusive relationship with her nineteen-year-old boyfriend. She continued her story: "I was just an eleven-year-old little girl, I didn't know what rape was, but my boyfriend, who was nineteen, brought me into a dark room and threw me on the bed and raped me. I didn't know what to do so I screamed, but no one heard me, like there was no one else in the world but me and him. I remembered that my mom had promised me that whenever I needed her, all I had to do was scream her name and she would come running. Where was she?" No one heard Angela crying out, not even her mom. Before this relationship ended her boyfriend shot her in the back and tried to kill her. She numbed her pain with alcohol, cocaine, smoking weed and crack. And she tried to kill herself several times.

She thought that by having sex with her boyfriends she was doing the right thing to find the love and acceptance that she longed for. In ninth grade she began to realize that the other kids were talking about her behind her back, calling her nasty names. Her self-image was ruined, but she knew that things had to change. About this time she met a boy who she thought was the one; he was her everything. She loved him with all her heart; she became pregnant and thought that everything was going to be good. Then she lost the baby and the relationship ended. Shortly after that, she came to Mega Youth with one of her friends.

When she finished telling her story, I asked everyone who had been addicted to come up to the front of the room to give Angela a hug. She was overwhelmed by the number of people who came up to hug her, and she told me that she realized that there were others out there who had experienced addictions at a young age like she had. She shared with me later that one girl came up to her and whispered in her ear, "I was eight when I first had sex, and hearing your story gives me courage that I can change, too."

One day Angela wrote to tell me, "Because of my sex addiction I just wanted to be invisible." Like so many other girls who have experienced the same desperation, she did not know how she would ever change her life or find herself in all this sadness and confusion. I always ask the kids why they keep doing this, why are they addicted. Why do they do it? They say it's because no one loves them. Where are their families? Where is the structure in their lives? Where is their home team made up of both family and friends?

Angela later told me that she was also on probation for violence. I laughed at her because she is five feet five and barely a hundred pounds. She said to me, "No, really, I am on probation for almost killing a girl. I broke her nose and sent her to the hospital and she almost died." This little girl had so much anger. Why? It was painful for me to listen to a story like Angela's, but then she told me that she now knows that God loves her and that she didn't want that bad life anymore. The pain I was feeling for her began to subside and I began to hope for her again.

Angela has begun the slow process of changing her life. She still has problems with her mom, she is tempted by sex, but now she has a community to fall back on, people to give her love and support when she is tempted. We won't let her fall back into her sex addiction. We have to love her and believe in her and care for her day by day, reminding her that God's love is always there to raise her up and remind her that she is amazing!

In 2007, she went to Soulfest in New Hampshire, a gathering of more than fifteen thousand youth featuring Christian music and speakers, and she shared her story with hundreds of people. She spoke to the large crowd with confidence and told them her story: "I was a sex addict and I was ruining my life, but now that I have come to Christ He has forgiven me. I am loved." Angela now understands that Christ loves her, and that is all that matters. She knows that we love her and believe in her and that with God all things are possible!

Angela plans to conquer her addictions. She wants to use her story to touch thousands of lives, to bring God's love to others. She wants to make an impact on this world like Christ made an impact on her life.

Angela Speaks

1. What was your home life like? Do you have brothers and sisters? Do you get along with your parents?

I didn't have a good relationship with my parents. They didn't really care about me or about what happened to me. I think that my mom tried to do the best things for me, but after she divorced my dad she went from one relationship to the other and that was what she focused on, not me. My sisters were mean to me and told me that I was adopted and that my parents really didn't want me. I had a different father than they did, so I think that they never really got me. My mom once told me that sex was something that you could give to a guy and so that's what I did.

2. When did you start having sex? What was your life like then?

I was ten years old the first time I had sex. For that brief time I felt like I was doing something that would make someone love me no matter what. Wrong! By the time I was eleven I was in a sexually abusive relationship where my boyfriend, who was nineteen, raped me and beat me. One day he shot me because he was out of control and the bullets hit me in the back and the leg. I recovered and left him and started a new relationship, which was more stable and supportive. I had been friends with the guy since I was ten. I really loved this guy and I stayed with him, but then he committed suicide. I couldn't believe it; it really hurt me down deep. Two years later I met a new guy and started having sex with him. I really loved him. I got pregnant and I thought that things would be OK then, but I lost the baby and then I lost him. I didn't know what to do.

3. What first inspired you to come to the Mega Youth Ministries?

I had heard about Mega Youth and I really needed some help. I had a bad self-image, and I knew that everyone was talking about me behind my back. So I decided to try it out. Justin told me that I was amazing, and the kids listened to me when I told my story.

4. How did you feel after you shared your story with other young people during the Mega Youth meeting?

At first I was not sure what to think. Justin was telling me that I was amazing, and these kids I didn't know were listening to me tell my story. I thought that they were just lying to me. How could they accept me for who I was when I didn't accept myself? Gradually I understood that I was finally at a place where I could be myself and I could feel the love of Jesus, and I felt happy.

5. Did people come and talk to you about your experience? Did people respond to you differently after you shared your story?

People came up to me after I told my story, and some of them said that they really understood because they had experienced something like what I went through. I did not feel like a "sexual addict"; I felt like a person who was loved and accepted. At first I kept waiting for someone to talk about me or tell me that I didn't deserve to be there, but it never happened. I knew that I had found the place where I would be able to become a better person and understand my problems so that I could do something about them. I have gone to Soulfest and I have been a leader at some of the retreats. I want to encourage people and help them the same way that everyone at Mega Youth has helped me.

6. How did Justin help you to prepare yourself to tell your story? What has his support meant to you?

Justin helped me by encouraging me and telling me that God loved me and that he knew that I was an amazing person who was meant to help other people. His support gave me the courage to tell my story at Soulfest, and everyone was so supportive and accepting of me there. I want to help other kids to see that they are amazing, and that God's love and the support of the Mega Youth community can help them as well.

7. Talk about the impact that God's love has had on your life. How did God's love bring you through this?

I live with my real father now, and although it has been tough, we have a good relationship now. It hasn't been so good with my mother. I find it difficult to trust my mom because she walked out on me and kept me from my real dad for so long. But I really do believe in relationships, and I feel that I can now have better relationships with people because I feel good about where I am in my life. I have become a leader in the Mega Youth group and I try to help others with their problems. My life is more focused and less intense than it was; I know that I am someone special and that by finding God's love and praying every day I can be a better person.

THE HEART OF THE MINISTRIES

Marisa's Story: Cutting

Justin Speaks

Marisa came to Mega Youth Ministries at age fifteen, ready to change her life and to stop her destructive behavior. She was looking for a miracle. Her life hadn't been easy. She was bulimic, a drug addict, and at the age of thirteen she had begun cutting herself with sharp razors. How had she gotten to this point?

She always felt like a failure at school and she had long lost her sense of hope. She had to go to summer school after failing in her classes. She hung out with the wrong kids in school because she thought it was "cool." She felt like her life was a complete mess.

Marisa's parents were divorced when she was young, her mother was an alcoholic, and her older brother and sister were just plain mean to her. Her sister hurt her, threw things at her, and said nasty things to her; basically her sister hated her and blamed her for their parents' divorce. Why? Marisa didn't know; she just figured it was because she was there, in the way. Her brother didn't treat her any better, but he didn't hate her as aggressively as her sister did. He told her one day, "Why don't you just kill yourself?"

She never felt good about herself, and she felt like nothing was ever going to change for the better for her; things just kept getting worse and worse. Without much support from her parents or the rest of her family by the seventh grade she had become a drug addict, developed bulimia, and was most certainly an alcoholic. In the midst of all of this misery she began cutting herself when she was alone, and no one was aware that she was doing it. Cutting herself was her way of trying to stop the pain of living by hurting herself.

The first night Marisa came to Mega Youth she walked up to the front of St. Charles Church asking for the love of God. She cried as she told us that she wanted to end her life. She hated herself; she hated her body and who she was trying to be, who she thought everyone wanted her to be. Then she met a guy who asked her to come to Mega Youth with him.

Now was her time to rise up and be healed; to realize that she was not a loser or a horrible person and that with God's love and the community of Mega Youth Ministries she might be able to change her life. Every week Marisa came to Mega Youth and talked about what a bad person she was and how ugly she felt. She felt like no one cared about her and that she might as well go cut herself or kill herself because she was worthless. Her sister told Marisa that until she was born her mother and father loved each other, but now they didn't get along at all. When Marisa was five years old her mother came home drunk and tried to kill her father in front of her. It pains me to hear stories like this, but I have to believe that with God anything is possible. We would have to find a way to let Marisa know that she was a wonderful person.

At fifteen Marisa had been through so much more than I had been through in my entire lifetime. Her heart was saying, I need love, Justin. How could we help her? It seemed that the only way to help her to find herself would be to make sure that she knew that she could do it, and for all of us to believe in her no matter how she felt about herself. She needed love and acceptance from God and from us so that she would be able to love and accept herself. I read one day that a great saint said, "Sometimes you need to love someone for two, three or maybe even ten years before you can tell them their faults." I believed we needed to do this with Marisa. She needed unconditional love bad.

As I often do with new members of Mega Youth, I asked her to write her life story for me, what she had gone through growing up. It was sixteen pages of pain. She came to Mega Youth with fresh scars on her wrists. When people who have been cutting themselves stop doing it, eventually they develop white scars on their wrists as they heal. Marisa's scars were not white. They were newly reopened and she had been bleeding. Marisa asked me, "Why me, Justin? Why do I cut my wrists? I want to stop." I needed an answer for her, and at that very moment God gave it to me. She needed the courage to share her story with everyone and to find the help and support that she needed in our community.

I told Marisa that I was so glad that she was alive, and that I knew that she didn't fully understand why she cut herself. "If you don't mind, I want to share something with you," I said.

She asked me what I wanted to share with her.

I told her that the Bible tells us that whatever "you do to the least of my brothers and sisters you have done to me." I asked her, "Marisa, are you Jesus's sister?"

"Yes," she told me in a quiet voice with her face down looking at her wounded wrists.

I told her to cut Jesus then.

She asked me what I was saying. "I can't cut Jesus," she said.

But I told her that she already had. "Marisa, every time you cut yourself you cut Jesus. So please stop cutting yourself, and always remember that God loves you very much."

Marisa found the magnificent Love of God that day and she has been growing and changing ever since. She stopped cutting herself, although she has struggled a few times. She found out that she could love and accept herself when she realized that her God loves her so much that He would suffer with her and for her. It has been so powerful to watch her love those who are hurting as deeply as she once did, and to watch her spend her time building others up.

She is still struggling to find her place in this world. She has to remind herself every day that she is a good and loving person in the eyes of God. I told her to love Jesus first because He will keep her focused on loving others and herself in an intense and powerful way.

Marisa now knows that we need to love who we are, and that it is not easy. Many times our thoughts and emotions get the best of us and we begin to doubt our self-worth. We think, Why me? Why do I have to go through this? No one understands. No one can relate to me. There are many people cutting themselves. They need someone to be real with them about why they are doing it so that they can heal themselves. Marisa has been the one to help Angela through her struggles, and Sammy (whom we will meet later in this chapter) is helping Angela and Marisa because they are sharing what they have been through, and that is what helps them to change.

Marisa Speaks

1. What was your home life like? Do you have brothers and sisters? Do you get along with your parents?

My mother is an alcoholic; for as long as I can remember she drank. Around the time I turned five she started cheating on my dad. My mother used me and I never trusted her. I have a brother and a sister but I am not very close to them either; they have always picked on me and made my life difficult. My sister would throw things at me when she was mad at me, and my brother just plain hated me. My dad was always there for me and I live with him now, but he travels for his job during the week. So basically I am alone a lot of the time.

2. Why did you cut yourself?

I wanted to hurt myself because my life wasn't worth much. I couldn't talk to my brother or sister because I just annoyed them; they didn't know who I was anyway. I felt that I could not turn my life around without some help, but who would ever help me? I wanted to feel something, and at least when I cut myself I felt pain.

3. What first inspired you to come to the Mega Youth Ministries?

When I was at the mall one day I met this guy who seemed really nice and he had a car. I could talk to him about my feelings, so I told him about the drugs and the cutting. One night he took me to the movies and afterward he confronted me about my problems and asked me to come to Mega Youth with him. They were doing Adoration at Mega Youth that night, but I had stopped believing in God when I was about ten, so I didn't know what to do.

4. How did you feel when you were asked to share your story with other young people during the Mega Youth Meeting?

At first I didn't want everyone to know about the cutting and the other problems I had. I didn't know what to do, so I dropped to my knees and begged God for forgiveness. At that point Justin asked me to talk about my bad week with everyone. I was so surprised that everyone was so accepting of me. Justin told me how amazing I was. No one had ever said anything like that to me before, and at first I figured that they would let me down, too. And sometimes I still struggle, but I feel that I have found a place for me. God knows who I am, and I feel that He understands what I am struggling with every day.

5. Talk about the impact that God's love has had on your life.

Prayer has helped me more than I could have known. I am so much more into prayer than I would have expected. God listens to me, and so do the people at Hard as Nails and Mega Youth. But mostly I listen to myself now, and I know that I am a worthwhile person. I am not scared of life like I was before. I have been a leader at Soulfest, which was intense. Everyone there showed their faith and was really into it. I feel that I have helped people by telling them my story. My brother talks to me now and sometimes watches out for me. Before he left for college he told me not to f—— up anymore. I have stopped cutting myself and I am focusing on God's love and helping others now.

Sammy's Story: Suicide

Justin Speaks

As a young child Sammy lived a chaotic and abusive home life in the suburbs. She was adopted, which should have been good for her, but her parents got divorced when she was young, which made her sad. When she was ten years old she was raped by her mother's boyfriend. When little Sammy told her mom what had happened, her mother didn't believe her and told Sammy that she was lying.

After the divorce, Sammy's relationship with her adoptive mother started to deteriorate. Her mother's second marriage was to a man who was verbally and physically abusive to Sammy (and also to her mother at times), and she and her mother fought constantly over this. One day Sammy's mother was so angry with her that she threw her in the lake and left her for dead. Shortly after that her mother divorced that husband and married a third one who was even more abusive than the previous two husbands. After one particularly terrible fight Sammy's mother kicked her out of the house for good. Even though her relationship with her mother was not great, now at fifteen, Sammy had lost her mother and wanted to die.

At this point she started cutting herself and then trying to kill herself. Even though her home life had been a mess, she loved her mother and missed her terribly. She didn't want to live anymore. Throughout all of this pain and suffering Sammy had lost touch with her original adoptive father, but after her mother kicked her out she found him and went to live with him.

When I met Sammy she was fifteen. I could see the pain in her eyes, but I could feel the childlike yearning in her heart that God gave her to overcome all the garbage she had experienced in her short life. When I work with young people I try to focus beyond the mess of their daily lives to see the person they could become one day. In Sammy I saw someone who could one day be a leader, showing people the way to God's love. The mess is not who she is but merely the life she was born into. Sammy is a gift from God, and she can use her story to shock the world into changing for the better. Will she change? Who knows? Can she change? Yes, I believe that one day this young girl could become a greater minister than me.

The first day I met her I asked her to be a leader in one of the skits we were going to perform at a Mega Youth meeting. She played a girl who was used by her boyfriend, had a mother who left her, and a friend who discouraged her. What I didn't realize at the time was that all of this was true in Sammy's life. Like the character she played, Sammy was addicted to drugs, drank often, and had a serious sex addiction. She had a confusing relationship with her mother, and many of her friends had not supported her when she needed them.

Even though she lived with her father, he traveled during the week so she was often left to fend for herself. And she was afraid of life until she met God the Father. I saw a bright shining light in her eyes; I couldn't see the pain. I could see only the love of Christ. It was awesome to watch this girl become such a confident, purehearted, caring, and beautiful young woman right before my eyes.

Even though she accepted God into her life, things didn't totally change right away for her; it took a while for her to commit to Christ. We spent many hours encouraging her to continue on and not give up when times got challenging. It was hard.

Her best friend was a guy named Joey; he was like an angel in her life. He would comfort her and encourage her when things really got bad for her, but he was killed in a car accident that winter after she had joined Mega Youth. Right after he died she went to a Mega Youth meeting with some of her friends who were very close to Joey. The Mega Youth community was there to support her when she needed us. The following summer she went on a weeklong camp with Hard as Nails. Being with everyone and talking with them about Joey gave her hope that with the love of God the Father, her relationship with Jesus Christ, and the power of the Holy Spirit she would keep moving ahead with her life.

She was beginning to become confident in her relationship with Christ and to understand the gift of communication she possessed. Then, in October of that same year, another close friend of Sammy's, Cory, committed suicide. I had a prayer service at the high school for the parents and youth in the area who were affected by Cory's death; the event enabled the community to come together to mourn for Cory and for her family to renew their hope and faith in the youth of Syracuse.

Over three hundred adults and young people came to share their pain that night, and I knew that God had me in Syracuse, New York for a reason. A few days later the school asked me to run an all-school retreat for about five hundred students to help them with the healing process. It was really a challenge.

Things were hard for Sammy; she was trying to renew her life in the love of Christ and these terrible things kept happening to her. It was a crossroads. Was Sammy going to understand through these experiences that the only love that is consistent is God's love for us? Or was she going to crawl back into herself? I knew that she needed time and space to make that decision for herself. It's so important when working with young people to give them the space and the time they need to make their own decisions.

Sammy became disillusioned by her faith community at Mega Youth; it felt fake to her now. It felt as though as soon as she got on her feet again something else bad was going to happen. At about the same time she attended a Hard as Nails retreat, and it was there that she gained valuable insight into the fact that God is alive and that if you count on Him you will be OK no matter what happens. Family and friends will come and go in your life, they may die or they may leave you, but God will always be there for you to rely on.

I remember quite vividly telling her, "You know why you can't give up."

"Why?" she asked.

"Because you are going to touch more lives with your life than I ever could."

She smiled and said, "Do you really think so? That is going to be a tough challenge."

I looked at her and I said, "I know so."

She nodded her head. YES! SAMMY WAS ON HER WAY TO GREATNESS!

She felt angry with life and had experienced a lack of hope, but she didn't give up on her faith. She kept fighting through the memories of her rape, her addictions, and her struggles with suicide. Sammy finally got to the point where she also believed that she was going to achieve greatness by touching other people's lives through God's love through her preaching.

Sammy preached with other young leaders with the Hard as Nails team. She spoke at many Wednesday night Mega Youth meetings; she helped with the confirmation retreats and traveled with us to run Hard as Nails events.

One night I had just gotten back from a Hard as Nails tour in New Jersey and I was totally exhausted, just plain worn out. I was supposed to be preaching that night, but I knew that I truly didn't have it in me to do the best job. So I talked to my team and asked them to preach for most of the event. I gave a brief message and then turned it over to the young people. I knew that I could count on all of them to do a terrific job of bringing God's love and understanding to the group at that event. I don't have to be the only one delivering the message. God uses all of us to give His message of love. They nodded their heads and they did a wonderful job, but no one shone as brightly as Sammy did that night.

She went up to the altar and asked the group, "How many of you feel like you can't do it?" Many of them raised their hands. She said again, "How many of you feel like you just want to end your life, like you want to give up?" Half of the group raised their hands. I remember her saying something like this: "I was raped and I am not going to give up because Jesus on that cross didn't give up on me. My family left me and I can't give up. One of my friends died in a car crash and another committed suicide, and I am not giving up. Jesus didn't go through all of that for you to give up, so why are you going to?" She closed with saying, "If I haven't given up after what I have been through, then you can do it too!"

Sammy put the microphone down and for about five seconds it was completely silent; the power of her words had made all of them think! I could hear people crying, and I started to pray deeply because I sensed similar pain among the young people attending. That night was Sammy's night. I knew then that Sammy had the gift to make a difference in many lives. I was so encouraged that God would let me see such a miracle. It was amazing to watch her; I know that one day she will touch more lives than I ever could. I asked Sammy what she wanted to do with her life, and she told me that she wanted to be a minister like me. I have always believed that it is not just what you do with your life that matters; it's also what those who follow after you do with their lives. How can I inspire more young people like Sammy to become strong leaders in their faith and to inspire others to find God's love?

Our story, our life, our challenges, our fears, our unique journey is a weapon of love, an arrow that can be directed to the hearts and souls of many. It is to be used carefully everywhere we go. Sammy has learned that her story is a treasure. We can't focus on how bad we are, how tough our life is, or how painful it may feel. We need to understand our horrible experiences as well as our joyful ones and share them with others so that they may know that we all are human and in need of a relationship with God.

Sammy Speaks

1. *What was your home life like?*

I was adopted but my parents got divorced when I was three years old. My mom married someone who was very abusive both verbally and physically. I loved my mom but I didn't understand how she could let him hurt us the way he did. Finally she divorced him and then she married another guy who was more abusive than her second husband. She blamed me for all the fights that he picked with me, so at fifteen she kicked me out of her house. She just told me to pack up and get out for good. I couldn't believe that I had lost my mom, and I tried to kill myself. I started cutting myself, too, and tried to kill myself again.

2. *Why did you try to commit suicide?*

I wanted to hurt myself because my life wasn't worth much then. My own mother did not even want me. I felt as though I was all alone and that no one wanted me, not my birth mother and not my adoptive mother either. I have had other people my age die; one of my friends committed suicide and another friend, Joey, died in an accident. I saw what it did to everyone around them. It hurt.

3. *What first inspired you to come to the Mega Youth Ministries?*

Some of my friends had been coming to the Mega Youth meetings and they liked them, so I thought that I would come too because they said that the people were very supportive. What I liked most was that it was a group of kids who have strong faith and are willing to really help you through whatever your problems are. Their support is unconditional and you feel accepted.

4. How did you feel when you were asked to share your story with other young people during the Mega Youth Meeting?

I feel like I am helping others when I tell my story at Mega Youth. I was still suicidal when I first came to Mega Youth, and by sharing my story I realized that I was worth something and that I had something to live for: helping others to find God's love. I got such positive feedback from everyone that it helped me feel better about myself. I have made good friends at Mega Youth and I can count on them if I am feeling sad. They helped me when my friend committed suicide and also when my friend Joey died.

5. Talk about the impact that God's love has had on your life.

I now have a positive relationship with my adoptive dad; he really is there for me. He supports my coming to Mega Youth, which is important to me. I feel that I have made a difference to the kids I tell my story to. I hope that I have helped them just like everyone helped me when I first came here. Through God's love I have learned to love myself and to accept myself, and it has made me care more about other people. I have brought some of my friends to Mega Youth and they have liked it too.

Marc's Story: The Loss of a Child

Justin Speaks

As I watched the five o'clock news on Channel 9 in Syracuse New York, one night I heard that a young boy named Aaron had died at age thirteen. It hit me hard. I thought about the boy's father and wondered how a father could bury his young teenage son. Seeing your son die would have to be a nightmare, even if it was in a hospital and he died of natural causes. Being a new father myself, it hit me; I prayed for that father that night and hoped that one day I would be able to meet him and help him through his grief.

Living in Syracuse, I have had a connection with both Bishop Ludden and Bishop Grimes high schools. I visit these high schools often as part of the Mega Youth Ministries, and I consider myself to be part of the school family. Shortly after I heard the story of the boy who had died I ran into the daughter of one of the Bishop Ludden employees; she seemed so sad. I asked her what was wrong, and she told me that her boyfriend, Aaron, was the boy who had just died. She and her mother invited me to the lunch that was being held at the local bar to help raise money to pay for the funeral and doctor costs. I was busy but I knew that I had to go so that I could meet Aaron's father, to let him know that I was praying for him. I sat there waiting for the chance to speak with him but it never happened; too much was going on that night. When I left I shook his hand and I wondered when I would have the chance to really meet him.

Thinking about family, I realized how important the bond

is between father and son. I love my own son so much that I couldn't imagine the pain and torture that this young father was going through.

I share my thoughts with my wife often; she just listens; she's a good sounding board for me. A few months after I heard the news about Aaron, my wife's cousin called to tell me about a friend of hers named Marc who needed my help. Since I rarely hear from her I couldn't figure out why she had called me. Mary just smiled and said, "You know Marc. He's the father you have been praying for and hoping to meet." WOW! God works wonders; I felt in my heart how much my God cares about those in need. I wanted to help Aaron's father, and now I was going to meet him and have the chance to do that!

I called Marc and asked him if he would like to go to lunch at my favorite spot in Syracuse, Tully's. When we met at the restaurant, I figured that Marc was maybe thirty-years old—and he had been the father of a thirteen-year-old. It was unbelievable to me that he was so young. He didn't know where to go, and even though I had no answers for him I could sit and listen to him and explain how the love of God could help him through this impossibly difficult time. He explained that his ex-girlfriend and he had conceived his son but that their relationship had not worked out. He shared with me that he had spent a lot of time with his son and that they had had a good relationship. He felt guilty that his relationship with his son's mother had not worked out and that his only son was gone. He told me that he wished that he could have done something to save his son; he felt helpless. Why hadn't the doctors been able to determine why he died? He wanted to believe that they could have done something to save him. Marc needed to heal and move on with his life and he needed the love of God to do it.

As we sat there eating I remembered that I had to go to New Jersey for some meetings later that week. I asked Marc then and there if he wanted to go to New Jersey with me, and he said yes immediately. I was surprised since I had only known him for an hour, but I thought that it would be a good chance for us to talk more. I knew that if I could talk with him I could help him to find his way. Later I called to let him know that we would be leaving on Thursday morning at five a.m. WOW! The father I had prayed for and had wanted to meet was now going to be driving to New Jersey with me, and we would have lots of time to talk. God does make a difference and he does work miracles.

I had decided to surprise Marc when I picked him up on Thursday. During our conversation I had learned that he was a big Yankees fan. Since we were going to have to attend a lot of business meetings and programs with people he didn't know, I had decided to take him to a Yankees game. To say that I am not a Yankees fan is putting it mildly because I am a true Cleveland Indians fan (not just the Indians but all of the Cleveland teams!). Any team with twenty-six world championships makes me sick since the Indians haven't won one since 1948. But I wanted this to be a special trip for him, so I decided that it was important to take him to see his team, to give him something to look forward to. I was secretly pumped anyway because he told me that he had never been to a game.

After all of the meetings ended we headed out to the game. I complained the whole time about how I couldn't root for Marc's team because, after all, they were the Yankees. After two innings, though, I felt horrible because the Yankees were losing 10–1 to the Texas Rangers. Cover your ears, Cleveland, because I actually felt bad for the Yankees, but more than that I felt bad for Marc. He finally gets to go to a Yankees game and they start losing BIG-TIME!

But the score didn't matter to Marc; he was having a good time and was actually laughing about the score. I started silently rooting for the Yankees, which is almost worse than a sin for me. Marc's smile and excitement started to get to me, and for the first time in my life I was hoping the Yankees would make a comeback. I sat in amazement that not only could God help me to meet Marc, but He could also get me to attend a Yankees game and root for the team I have always loved to hate.

Three hours and forty-nine minutes later I looked up at the scoreboard and the score was 13–12 with the Rangers still leading. I was thinking, Come on, Yankees, come on Yankees! Jorge Posada was at the plate with two outs and one man on. I thought to myself, God, you are giving Marc incredible grace right now. I believed his son, Aaron was in heaven and Marc was going to get his answer that everything would be all right now. *SMACK!*—Jorge Posada blasted one to the bleachers and the Yankees won the game. We ended up being at the Yankees' biggest comeback game in their illustrious history. It was amazing; that is all I have to say, and we were there. God was there. Marc went home with the biggest smile on his face knowing that the Yankees had won despite terrible odds and that there was a God who loved him, his son, and his family.

Whenever I feel down or I start thinking that no one cares, all I need to do is remember that God cares for the big things but He also cares for every little thing as well. I remember Marc smiling after that game. I think of the unbearable pain he has experienced and I remember how it all started. One prayer made a difference. By taking the time to reach out, to spend time with someone in pain, I made an impact on my life and on his. Taking a new friend to the ball game touched our hearts forever and gave him some happiness amidst the sadness of the loss of his son. And it reminded both of us of the depth of God's love.

Marc Speaks

1. What, if any, addictions have you struggled with in your life?

I have struggled with alcohol in the past, and it became worse when my son died. I was trying to use drinking to deaden the pain. The alcohol was just making me more depressed.

2. What was your first reaction when you met Justin Fatica?

When I first met Justin I was a little taken aback because of how intense he can be about his faith. After spending a short time with him I saw that his heart is filled with love for everyone, and his intensity became comforting.

3. How has your relationship with Justin helped you to deal with the tragedy of losing your son?

My relationship with Justin has helped me deal with the loss of my son. I am able to share my story with others and let them know that no matter what happens things can get better. Helping others is helping to ease the pain in my heart.

4. Have the doctors discovered yet what your son's illness was?

The doctors say we will never know for sure what happened. The final determination was unexplained natural causes.

5. Have you ever attended one of the Hard as Nails events? If so, what did you think?

I have attended several Hard as Nails events and I'm amazed each time at how the youth and adults open their hearts and share about their trials and fears.

6. How has God's love brought you through this experience?

God's love has helped me in that He has sent hundreds of amazing people into my life to share with me, laugh with me, and cry with me. Mostly just having someone who is there for me if I need to talk has helped me.

7. What was your trip to New Jersey with Justin like?

My first trip to New Jersey was truly a blessing. I met some people I can call true friends. But the highlight was the Yankees game. I love the Yankees even though Justin doesn't. I was thrilled because I had never gone to a major league game and the first one was a Yankees game. When they were down eight runs at the start of the second inning I thought, Great, my first game and the team's getting killed. As they slowly came back I was becoming more excited. I truly believe it was God and my son who helped the Yankees win and made me forget my problems for that little bit of time. I think of that game almost every day, and when I do I smile because I know I have someone watching me.

8. How are things for you today?

I'm still struggling, but I know support is just a phone call and a prayer away. I know the pain and hurt will never truly leave, but without Jesus in my life I don't think I would have the strength to live a positive life.

Chapter Five

THE FUTURE OF THE HARD AS NAILS MINISTRIES

*"No one has greater love than this, to lay down
one's life for one's friends. You are my friends if
you do what I command you."*

Jn 15:13–14

I don't know what my future holds for me. One of the most accurate sayings I've ever heard is If you want to make God laugh, tell him your plans. He has greater plans for all of us than we could ever dream of for ourselves, so why go crazy trying to control things? In life I need to have goals, visions, hopes, and a mission. But for my spiritual life I only know one thing: I need to love the Lord with all my heart, soul, and strength and love all people no matter what their stance or view. Proverbs 3:5–6 says, "Trust in the Lord with all your heart, on your own intelligence rely not; In all your ways be mindful of him, and he will make straight your paths."

The Ministries are where God calls me now, but that is today. When I say things like "This is what is going to happen" I think that is not fair to me or anyone else. That is limiting God's greatness. God will do far greater things with the Ministries that I run than even I can fathom or imagine. I will share what I hope God will do through us.

Have you ever heard of an unordained Catholic minister? Have you ever met a young man or woman who has given his or her life to the Catholic Church who is not a priest or a religious brother or sister? I have not received the sacred call to the priesthood. I do not desire a powerful role in my church. I only want to help assist the church in bringing young people back into the fold. Will it happen? It's beginning to happen now but it may take more than my lifetime to be fully realized, and that is OK. I have my own style and sometimes that works for me and sometimes it works against me, but everything I do is in His name and with His Love. But the good news is that there are others who are being trained who will do it. We will rally our young people and get them involved with their parishes or churches. The goal is to build a large enough base of young people so that the Catholic Church will have hope for the future.

God has called me to build a community with a small group of people (the ministers who work with Hard as Nails, the youth leaders involved with Mega Youth Ministries), a local community of people (Mega Youth Ministries), and a global group (Hard as Nails Ministries) who work together for this common goal. Mega Youth is the local program and although many blessings have come, it has proven to be challenging at times. The Syracuse people have taken a stand in realizing the need for building this youth program. On a weekly basis we have young people and adults who come to receive the message of Jesus Christ. This is because of the Syracuse community—these people have been a gift from God for me. It is always harder to build community in the city where you live, but little by little I am seeing the community respond to the needs of the Syracuse youth. It is amazing to see how many young people are in need and how many want to build a relationship with Christ. We have had over a thousand different young people come to Mega Youth since we started in October of 2005.

The challenge of Mega Youth remains with rural, sub-urban, and inner city young people coming together. Most parents want to be comfortable with the surroundings and programs their children are involved in, and reaching out to all people is definitely intimidating at times, even for me. Since young people are suffering so much, as you have learned, it is hard for a lot of people to be real with what is truly going on with our youth in America. The young people who come to Mega Youth meetings to share their life stories with us are from different socioeconomic backgrounds. A number of parents in the suburbs express concerns over their children being exposed to the problems and hardships of some of the youth who share their needs and difficulties at the Mega Youth meetings. It never ceases to amaze me that many of the parents who express these concerns have children who have shared hardships, addictions, and struggles that the parents may not be completely aware of. This is a tremendous challenge for our ministry.

Many of the people from the community come to me and want to know where all the kids from the parish are. It's tough to state the obvious—that there are few kids going to church today—but it's the sad truth! We need to reach out and love all people so they will see that they are important to the church, Christ is important, and the Catholic Church is important. So who are the parish kids? I believe all God's children are.

Mega Youth Ministries has many challenges, but the much needed help that this community of young people is receiving from the Ministries far outweighs the difficulties that we might face along the way. Many of the young people we minister to have been healed through the love of Jesus Christ by the outstanding adult leaders who lead Mega Youth. The community that Mega Youth provides has saved a lot of kids who have suffered from cutting, rape, suicide, ignorance, disrespect, addictions, racism, despair, and loneliness. Hundreds of young people have had the courage to face their problems, and that is why we want to build the Ministry.

Many priests have told me to continue my work "because there are many programs like yours in the Protestant churches, but we need this now."

Honestly I am not sure what God has in store for us, but I hope that the people of Syracuse will rally around the mission of Mega Youth and we will be able to build the first arena for young people as a community gathering place. This arena would seat five thousand to ten thousand people. As we build more in other cities, the size will fluctuate depending upon the needs of the city that we are ministering to. Under the auspices of the Hard as Nails Ministries we would build arenas in other cities that embrace the Ministries and build their own Mega Youth groups. The arenas would be state-of-the-art workout facilities and include other activities for youth eighteen years or younger. The kids would be able to use the facilities at the arena by attending a one-hour afterschool session with one of our mentors. Our mentors would help them with their school work and then share with them their faith in God.

The funding for such projects will have to come from people who are willing to support a facility that they can believe in, a facility that will provide activities they want their children and the youth of each community to be able to take advantage of whenever possible.

In Barbados we have begun to build another Mega Youth–type program called The Movement. In June 2006 five Hard as Nails ministers came to the island to preach in public schools and at churches so that the The Movement could build its own youth group. There are not many weekly youth groups on the island, so we took great joy in the reality that we built this one and it is still going strong. The priest who runs the seven Catholic churches on Barbados gave us his blessing to build The Movement in Barbados and make it the base for the future Caribbean mission. Since there is no bishop on the island right now he acts as the leader for the island.

Recently we went back to Barbados for the wedding of one of the Hard as Nails ministers and the woman who helped us to build the Barbados movement. Many adults who live on other Caribbean islands attended the wedding. They were so impressed by what God had done through the

Hard as Nails Ministries in Barbados that they reached out to us. Now church leaders from Saint Kitts, Saint Lucia, and Trinidad want us to build Hard as Nails Ministries on their islands.

How did we build such a successful mission in Barbados? It was through the amazing efforts of Tim Hanley, one of my former students who was involved with the campus ministry at Paramus Catholic. That is why I am a firm believer that it is not about what we do, but about those who come after us. I am nothing compared to those who will follow after me. Leaders building leaders is what I believe is most important as we move forward.

The future of Hard as Nails is going to be interesting, but if I trust in the Lord and give my whole heart to love others, He will do the impossible. God has plans for me and He has plans for you. Be part of the Hard as Nails Ministries by helping to build your youth community, being a volunteer with Hard as Nails or another youth program. Join a Hard as Nails tour in an area near you, pray for us, and, most important, bring the message of Hard as Nails to your family by using the information included in this book. Doing these things will help you and your family to think deeply about how you can become a better Christian and how you can live out your faith in beautiful ways. When it is over it is over, but what we share with our families, friends, and the world can live on forever.

Remember it is not about what we do, but about who we are!

YOU ARE BEAUTIFUL! YOU ARE UNIQUE! and YOU ARE AMAZING!

Thoughts on the Future by Father Bryan Page, Spiritual Advisor to
Hard as Nails Ministries

My first introduction to Hard as Nails was through Brian
Greenfield. We met at Seton Hall University. I walked into a
very large event on campus late one night, and at the door, as
he was leaving, Brian grabbed a basketball player and began
to pray with him. I remember thinking that it was an impres-
sive sight, this six-feet-nine campus basketball star praying
with this five-feet-eight campus minister. The scene really
opened my eyes to the fact that many people want to know
God, and that we cannot be ashamed to approach them and
help with the introduction. A few years later Ichiro Kawasaki from the Hard as Nails Ministries was sent by God to
call me to pray when I needed it most.

Within the Hard as Nails Ministries I play somewhat of
an advisory role in helping them to navigate through some
potential spiritual and practical pitfalls. The Ministry has the
potential to grow from a few ministers affecting many lives
to a coordinated effort, reaching into the lives and hearts of
all whom they touch, and in turn, providing them with an opportunity to share their lives and touch others. In the future
I see more men and women becoming active in their faith
through Hard as Nails, embracing the promise they made at
baptism and confirmation, to share the Gospel. I pray about
my part in the sacramental ministry and spiritual guidance
of those involved with the Ministry. Justin's spiritual journey has provided the basis for the vision of the Ministry; his
story and experiences are powerful, and he has been called
to live his faith and fulfill his baptismal promises more fully

than most people I have met along the way. This serves as constant encouragement to me that our lives are a work in progress, and the most important thing that we work on is our ability to love.

I think that the Hard as Nails Ministries has the potential to bring many people to faith through love. There is a consistent message conveyed through all who work with the Ministries, whether in word or action, that every person on the planet is important, because God made them and loves them. And so long as we are on this planet, we can never put ourselves outside of His love. When people hear this message in their heart, lives change. No amount of punishment or discouragement can change the heart; they can only modify actions. But God's love can make anyone whole, so they can live for Him and the peace He offers.

Thoughts on the Future by Brian Greenfield, Minister with Hard as Nails Ministries

I met Justin at Seton Hall University when we were both students. We were in a prayer group that evolved into a retreat ministry called the 12 Apostles program. After graduation I went to Ohio for graduate school, and then I entered religious life with a Franciscan community in New York. I eventually left the community, but I had kept in contact with Justin throughout that entire time. I eventually moved back to New Jersey to work and finish graduate school. When I hooked back up with Justin he mentioned the Hard as Nails Ministries and asked me if I was interested. Ever since then I have been part of it.

I am an event coordinator; I lead retreats and speak at various Hard as Nails events. I have been living and working with a group of urban youth in the Washington, DC, area and recently I have been doing a lot of work with black Catholics. I know that being a black male has a major role in all of this, so I guess that this has become my role in the Hard as Nails Ministries.

I always knew that there was a struggle in the church as far as diversity, but I have seen the hope and pain that other black Catholics feel about the church. I have seen how we want to do good things in the Catholic Church, but we don't know exactly what to do, and very few people come to the aid of these churches. It is discouraging at times because I have seen churches that have everything they want, and I have seen urban churches that solely have the hope and the love of the parishioners. I have a mixed feeling of anger, hope, and motivation. I feel for the people I speak to because I can relate to the struggles they are going through.

Justin has had the biggest effect on the way that I do ministry. He really made the faith come alive for me, and it was because of his leadership that I even got into my faith. The Hard as Nails style of ministry is all that I know because when I first got into my faith I was with Justin. I think Justin is kind of like my internal parent when it comes to ministry. I often think about how he would handle a situation. Being involved in ministry with Justin has also stretched my vision of ministry and I have seen its importance in bringing hope to people.

The future of the Hard as Nails Ministries is a bit of a mystery to me. The one thing that everyone involved in the leadership of the Ministries has in common besides our friendship is the desire for holiness. I envision success for the Ministries, but a lot of what we are doing with the youth has not been done in the Catholic Church before. There are many lay ministers in the church, but there are few lay ministries that consist of numerous professional lay ministers. So I don't have a clear vision of what success would look like.

I see the vision for the Ministries to be ministries that can appeal to people at different stages of life. We should be ministries that can bring hope to youth and adults. We have to be ministries that can meet people where they are but inspire them to desire holiness. We also have to challenge people to step out of their comfort zones and become the people that God calls them to be, beyond what other people have said that they are. Practically, I hope that we will be able to do ministry as a profession and still be able to take care of our families. My part in this vision is to bring the Lord's message of Love and acceptance, in the Hard as Nails way, to the groups of people that He wants me to inspire. Since I am a black Catholic and I am a young male, I have had a lot of opportunities to minister to the black Catholic Church as well as other urban groups. There is not one type of Hard as Nails minister; I must use my own unique gifts to be able to work effectively within my community.

Thoughts on the Future by Jeff Galletly, Board Member, Hard as Nails Ministries

I first met Justin when he did an event at my high school at the end of my freshman year. I thought (and continue to think) he was loud, arrogant, obtrusive, raw, and otherworldly engaging. He said those things that others thought, but then shied away from making public because of social filter, fear, common sense, or some aggregate of the preceding.

Magnetized not necessarily by Justin but by his ideals and his foundation, I became increasingly engaged in conversation with him, which was really his clamoring to obtain a potential soul (not in the "add another notch to the belt" sense) and telling, showing, living, and breathing with me the idea that I had value beyond academics, athletics, leadership, and wealth. But didn't that sum up everything I needed?

Since then I've become increasingly engaged with the reality of faith and of purpose, beyond the "things" I think I need. Beginning at the end of my freshman year of high school and carrying through to today, with many peaks and valleys in both faith and level of activity with Hard as Nails Ministries, I became involved in the beginning because of those magnets and that sense of value and that relentless clamoring that Justin gave me then and continues to give me today.

In short, I started hanging around Justin and was transformed by a living faith expressed through love. Although I am a board member and loathe saying this against our growth strategy, Justin is Hard as Nails; he breathes and bleeds it. To be around him is to be involved.

My vision for the future of the Ministries is the same youth-life-impacting vision of the past, only with greater efficiency and scale. Our executive director, Tim Hanley, has begun to set protocol for Hard as Nails Ministries to achieve such efficiency and scale without losing any of the positives that were around when we were still in our infancy: love, care, integrity, compassion, stewardship, friendship, family. These things remain.

As the Ministries grow and flourish, I will continue my work as a board member. I've been blessed to have the opportunity at a young age to work with such amazing people in a board setting. I believe that my involvement in the Ministry has benefited my faith; it has also benefited my personal and professional development as I further understand what is critical to leadership, communication, responsibility, and direction.

It is my hope and goal that the Hard as Nails Ministries will press forward in ecumenical love and the life-changing, ferociously positive, and powerful manner that got all of the media wheels turning. One would be hard-pressed to find a more worthy job that needs to be done than building up the youth of this world today through God's Love. The Hard as Nails Ministries is a tangible, multipurpose tool capable of chipping away scabbed and hardened lives and planting seeds of love, hope, and forgiveness.

Stepping on my soap box for just a second, there is a crisis in our world that will take people like Justin and Tim and others involved with Hard as Nails Ministries to confront, people who can look at folks like me or a youth hurting on the street and know that this person needs to be cared for and that there is another way to live life. We live in a world where our young people are in crisis mode every day. Abuse is a crisis. Suicide is a crisis.

Although each experience is different, Hard as Nails Ministries has taken on this life and continues to mold, shape, and refine it. Each of us has crises. Hard as Nails Ministries teaches us to go beyond our own existence and to reach out to others through God's Love and understanding.

Thoughts on the Future by Thomas Churchill Jr., Benefactor, Hard as Nails Ministries

I became involved with the Hard as Nails Ministries in my freshman year of high school at Paramus Catholic when Justin and his group came to the school and did an event. We were expecting it to be just another regular, boring retreat. Much to my surprise I entered the auditorium and saw a guy in his mid-twenties, screaming and doing push-ups with his theme song "Rocky," blaring through the speakers. Justin was an instant hit among all of the students, as we had never expected to see such things taking place at a Catholic high school retreat. By the end of the retreat, the display of love mixed together with Justin's intensity had the students buzzing for days about how much the retreat had helped them to understand God's Love for them.

Not long after the retreat Justin, this crazy twenty-three-year-old college student who had run the retreat, became a regular in the hallways at our school. He had become a religion teacher at Paramus Catholic High School. After a while though, the student body became split in their perception of Justin and his teaching methods. I was one of the many students who thought Justin was doing a great thing, but I didn't want to talk about my faith. As high school went on Justin seemed to always be around, and the most annoying thing about this was that his mission never changed and he never calmed down. He was a constant in the halls of our school from my freshman year to my senior year, which is when my first personal interaction with Justin finally took place.

During one of my free periods I got a group of friends together and waited outside his classroom for him to come out. Three of my friends and I tried to jump him, but it was a useless effort because he ended up fighting all of us off easily. Later that day I saw Justin at lunch; first he forgave me for my actions earlier in the day, and then proceeded to tell me how much he believed in me and that I could make a difference. From that day forward I would refer to Justin as a friend.

A year after graduating from high school I went back to Paramus Catholic to see the football team's opening game. I ran into Justin and we talked about how each of us had been. Then out of nowhere, Justin invited himself to my house to watch some NFL games. After a quick hesitation, I wondered why one of my high school teachers would be asking to come over to my house. Once we arrived at my house, Justin reminded me that he believed in me and that I could do great things.

He invited me to a prayer night at Paramus Catholic. As it turned out, that prayer meeting was one of the most inspiring events of my life. After that I attended every Hard as

Nails retreat I could get to, even getting some of my friends involved. It was then that I realized that I was called to be a part of Justin's ministry and I really started living my faith.

I spent a great deal of time with Justin and his ministry as he guided me through the beginning phases of my changing my life. To this day I thank Justin for being such an important part of my life. He is one of my best friends, and his ministry has changed not only my life but the lives of thousands of young people.

Within the Hard as Nails Ministries one of my jobs is to enable the growth of the Ministry through donations and other types of fund-raising. I am building contacts who believe in our goals as a ministry and are willing to be a part of it by helping with various donations, since the Hard as Nails Ministries are nonprofit. That being said, my vision for this ministry is continued growth and amazing success in changing the lives of the world's youth. It is impossible to be around people who are as enthusiastic and encouraging as the leaders of this ministry and not become part of the movement to make a positive impact on people's lives.

Thoughts on the Future by Ichiro Kawasaki, Minister with Hard as Nails Ministries

I first met Justin when I was a volunteer youth minister for a parish in the Archdiocese of Newark. Justin was campus minister for Paramus Catholic (a Catholic school in the archdiocese) at the time. We ran into each other at various events but never really talked or became close until a couple of years later. At an Archdiocese of Newark retreat, where the New York Giants were the keynote guests, I shared my story about how God had touched my life. Justin and some of his students—many of whom were the first youth to be involved with Hard as Nails—did a skit that featured Justin getting beat up by "sins" that were actually guys dressed up in T-shirts with the name of the sin written on them.

I was moved to tears by the message of the skit—how sin beats us down and keeps us oppressed, and how Jesus heals us, forgives us, and sets us free from sin. Sin hurts, but Jesus saves. I could relate to that because in my life I had struggled with so much sin which led to nothing but destruction and I was learning that Jesus could save me from that hurtful behavior. I also was amazed by the passion with which Justin spoke about Jesus. It was so obvious to me how much Justin loved God.

I was just starting to really live my faith at the time, and this was really inspiring for me—seeing a young man, my age, who was boldly living for the LORD with all his heart. I ran into Justin again at another Archdiocese of Newark retreat that I was helping to run. This time Justin gave a talk with Mary (now his wife, but not at the time) working as the sound technician on a boom box that blared rap music before Justin's talk. Again, I was moved by Justin's talk about living for Jesus and avoiding those sinful things that hurt God and us.

I also was amazed to see how Justin's direct and creative approach to ministry inspired young people. I had never seen a style so effectively reach the youth. And the youth were inspired to live for Christ and wanted to change their lives for the better!

How could I not want to become involved with something like that? I started helping Justin out at retreats and was an original member of the board of directors. I also was a big advocate along with Glynnis Woolridge (our first board president) for Hard as Nails becoming a nonprofit organization so the Ministry could touch more teens' lives! I always believed that God would use Hard as Nails in BIG ways, ways we never thought possible. In addition I've also helped as a Hard as Nails lay minister at various events, most recently traveling to Barbados for a Hard as Nails mission trip, through which I met my wife, Natasha! She lived in Barbados and arranged for Hard as Nails to come to Barbados through a mutual friend of ours named Brian Pedraza, who was formerly head of the Hard as Nails ministry for college students.

My life has been positively impacted by the incredible brothers and sisters in Christ that I've met through my involvement with Hard as Nails—most important, my wife. I've had the blessing of meeting a community of brothers and sisters who genuinely care about me and who have helped me to grow closer to God. Nothing has been more satisfying than our direct outreach to young people, helping them to know that God loves them and cares for them. Young people are going through so much today. They are hurting and they need God. Just sharing our experiences with them about how God has helped and saved us during difficult times is a great encouragement to them. It gives them hope and lets them know that they are loved by God.

Through my involvement with Hard as Nails I've learned

the truth that God's ways are not our ways. I would never have imagined that an HBO documentary film would be made about Hard as Nails or that the Ministries would be invited to do international mission trips for youth. Yet the documentary came out in December 2007 and we have just completed our second international mission trip. God leads and guides this Ministry. We just need to seek God in prayer, trust Him, and keep serving His people. He will take care of the rest.

Chapter Six

THE LETTERS

Then Jesus approached and said to them, "All
power in heaven and on earth has been given
to me. Go, therefore, and make disciples of all
nations, baptizing them in the name of the Father,
and of the Son, and of the holy Spirit, teaching
them to observe all that I have commanded you.
And behold, I am with you always, until the end of
the age."

Mt 28:18–20

Our young people are learning how to respect themselves
and others. They talk about tough topics and coura-
geously share their feelings with many different people.
They are learning how to do this at such a young age; it's
something that adults may take years to be able to do, if they
ever can. And they are learning how to share what has hurt
them the most, how to build themselves back up so that they
can move on. Many of them go to their parents to share what

has hurt them. Some even share with their parents how they have hurt them.

In addition to the sharing that takes place at the Hard as Nails events, many young people write letters to us telling us about their lives, problems, concerns, and sometimes they just tell us how much one of our events has meant to them. Since many of you reading this book may never be able to attend one of the Hard as Nails events, we thought that we would share with you some of the letters we have received. We have included several different examples of letters we have received in the hope that you will find one or more that you can relate to.

Read through the letters that we have included in this chapter; with each letter there is a response from me and a call to action. The call to action is designed to give the reader steps to take to help someone they know who is experiencing what the letter writer experienced. You should think creatively about how you can reach out to your church, strangers, friends, but, most important, to your family.

I believe that the most challenging dilemma that we face in America today is the breakdown of our beautiful families and stable home lives. These letters offer you a way to build your family back up. No matter what challenges your family has been through, these letters can help you to know that others have gone through similar challenges and that God has helped them to put the pieces back together again. It is our hope that these letters will provide you with the opportunity to start a dialogue of your own with either your parents or, if you are a parent, with your child.

Maintaining open lines of communication is one of the

most important things that we stress at the Hard as Nails events. It is so powerful and intense to witness a young person finally telling their story to a group of people who may or may not have experienced the same thing. By sharing their own stories, they are opening the way for others in the group to share their stories also.

It is my hope that by sharing these letters, you will open a dialogue with your loved ones about your life. I believe that we need to communicate with our family. Adults need to know what is going on with young people, and young people need to know that adults go through challenges, too. We need to get back to the reality that there is a right and wrong way to live our lives; we need to strive to live surrounded by God's love. It is wrong to get drunk or to drink underage; the Bible says so and parents should say so. Do we live by this? I don't know, but I really do hope so. If an adult swears and uses vulgar language out of anger, should that person care about how it affects other people? Is it wrong? Yes, the Bible says so, and why would we want to use any language that is discouraging?

So many young people follow the examples of their parents and other adults in their lives, but many adults do not even feel bad if they make mistakes like these, even though they negatively affect the young people in their lives. Some adults may not even think that these are mistakes or that the Bible and our faith in Jesus Christ should be taken seriously. I have included a chapter of letters that I have received from different young people, so that they can understand how to communicate, not proselytize, with adults and so that adults can focus on better communication with young people without lecturing them.

Everywhere I go I pay attention to what I do and what I say and how I say it. When I do something wrong I want to apologize for it. Some adults will not and cannot do that. My goal is not to have to apologize for anything, but since I am human I usually have to in some way every day. I joke with my wife and say every morning that I should apologize for things that I am going to do during the day. Do I want to hurt anyone? No, but I know that anything that I do to discourage someone in their faith could lead them into a destructive life, and I would never want to do that because I know how it feels.

Reading and reflecting on this chapter should give you the opportunity to really think about who you want to be or how you want to change for the better. Think about how you can get this book to someone who needs it. Reach out to a friend, a loved one, or an enemy. Yes, I said "enemy" because these are the people we should love most. I believe so strongly in outreach because of the difference that it has made in my own life. If Father Larry had never reached out to me, someone he found difficult and challenging, I never would have taken the path to God and this Ministry. He gave his love and guidance to me even when he thought the least of me, when I was making his life miserable. Now is the time and you are the one!

How can you benefit from using this book?

1. Read one of the following letters to someone out loud. It is a way to personally touch their life without having to be too personal.

2. Write your own letter and send it to someone you love so that you can tell them how you feel or what they are doing that hurts or helps you in your life.

3. Share a letter with someone who is going through the same thing that the person who wrote the letter was experiencing. Pick a letter that can touch that person's heart. Every letter is uniquely different as we all are in our life experiences.

4. Write your own letter and send it to me, Justin Fatica, and I will respond to you.

5. Create a group to work on *Hard as Nails* together.

6. Start a Bible study or prayer group and use *Hard as Nails* together. It will make a positive impact on your lives.

It is time to reach out to each other!

Letters to Hard as Nails Ministries

Cutting

"A thief comes only to steal and slaughter and destroy; I came so that they might have life and have it more abundantly." **Jn 10:10**

Dear Fatica,

I've seen so much pain in my life. I was molested and raped, and every time I used to close my eyes I would see those moments repeat over and over again in my mind. The pain didn't end there; boys and family have verbally and sexually abused me. I tried to run from all of this and went to drinking and drugs but they didn't help, so I went to the next best thing, cutting. Cutting became my life. I used to do it three to five times a week. One time I even put my arm under a running faucet so the blood wouldn't clot, but then I passed out. I hated myself and all of the pain that I went through; but then I met Jesus, and He changed my life. One of my friends took me to her youth group, and ever since then I haven't cut myself, and instead of picking up a knife I pick up a Bible.

Justin's Response

I am so sorry for the pain this world has caused you, but I am glad that the Lord has saved you.

Don't think for one minute that you will never again have horrible thoughts. Horrible thoughts will come back to you and they may try to haunt you. You'll have to continue to ask Jesus to calm your mind with His great gift of words, the Bible.

The Bible is the key to who you are. While the Lord is life, the energy of addiction and temptation are from the Evil One. Defeat that energy with the great gift of the Bible, for the Bible is the true source of positive power.

Also look to the help of friends who have been through similar situations, friends who have been successful in their lives. Pray for the help of someone older, thirty or forty years of age, who has achieved success through a positive attitude.

Also don't be so self-righteous that you think that atheists, Muslims, Hindi, or Christians from other denominations can't help you to live a positive life. I have learned some of the greatest lessons of self-respect and unselfishness from my Indian brother who practices his Hindi faith. In fact, my brother Ravi is one of the greatest gifts of love in my life. I want Ravi to know that every time I meet someone who reminds me of him, I find a positive power inside me that gives me the strength to be a better witness of Jesus Christ.

Look, search, and pray. Lean on people who will not hurt you but rather will help you achieve your dreams. If your dreams seem impossible to achieve, find people who can help you achieve them, and have faith in Jesus Christ. Make the impossible possible.

A Call to Action!

1. If you are sexually abused or raped, tell a family member and counselor immediately.
2. Ask yourself what unbearable pain you have been through. Then write a letter to a trustworthy friend. Tell them what you are going through and why you are going through it.
3. Pray that you can change, and then share your story with others who are struggling with cutting. Tell them that you believe that they can change, too. Remind yourself that you are not alone.

No One Likes Me

If God is for us, who can be against us? **Rom 8:31**

Dear Justin Fatica,

My whole life I was never really appealing to the world. I would try with makeup, nail polish, designer clothing, and jewelry, but I just never looked like one of those pretty girls. I was always called names like shorty, twig, ugly, and others. When I used to hear that I would try to cover up my pain and tears with a smile, so that no one would see that I was hurt, but inside I was dying! I would start to cry during school, and that would make me feel even worse. I felt like no one liked me, and that I would never fit in anywhere.

But then I met a preacher, and he told me that I was a beautiful child of God. He told me that every day until I began to believe it. Now I don't care what others think about me, because God is the only one who will truly judge me. I see others being made fun of, teachers and other kids in school, and now I have the courage to stand up for them. Now I'm striving to live for Christ, and I always remember that I'm a child of God, no matter what others might say!

Justin's Response

What a positive attitude you have! God has blessed you with the beautiful idea that God's magnificent love is the only way to survive in this judgmental, ignorant world. I am so impressed by people like you who can stand up to a world that defames or criticizes them.

Why does it matter if you look or act like everyone else? When God is on your side, the only thing that matters is that you impress Him. Impressing God is so free and refreshing, because He loves you just the way you are. God doesn't need us to look or act like everyone else. He only wants us to improve ourselves, improve our attitudes and behavior. No matter who you are, you can strive to change and improve yourself.

The world can be disheartening. It wants us to change ourselves in ways we can't change and to look "hot," or as good as movie stars. That can't happen, and God wouldn't want that to happen. He made you look the way you are for a reason. Know who you are, and don't try to be who you can't or shouldn't be.

Remember, God wants us to love Him, to love others, and to love ourselves. That is what is most important. When God wants you to win, He wants to make you better. He wants to improve you, your family, your friends, your enemies, and everyone else. Whose team do you want to be on, the ignorant world's team or God's team?

A Call to Action!

1. Look in a mirror and say, "If no one likes me, that means God doesn't like me, and that is a lie."
2. Write down the names of people who don't like you. Then write down those who do like you. Pray for the people on both lists.
3. What are your goals? Write them down. After you list them, ask God for help in achieving the most important goal. God wants you to work toward the goal that seems impossible!
4. If you ever get jealous of people, spend time with them in prayer. Try your best to be their friend. Don't hate them. Be around them and believe in them. Thank these people for their gifts.
5. Find people whom you think no one likes. Hang out with them, not as a "pity party" but because you know, in your

heart, what it feels like when no one likes you. Maybe you're wasting your time focusing on yourself and you need to spend time believing in other people.

Suicide

Let us then pursue what leads to peace and to build-ing up one another. **Rom 14:19**

Dear Justin,

When I was in the fourth grade I started thinking about suicide. This was attributed to the fact that basically my entire life my parents, particularly my father, drilled it into my mind that I was the biggest regret of their life. I was a mistake, an accident; because of me, both of their lives were totally ruined. I was completely useless and an utter disappointment. I started to blame myself for everything that went wrong. I blamed myself for my parents' marital problems (though my father never laid a hand on me, I know that he used to abuse my mother). I didn't have any positive support or encouragement in my life, so I started to cut myself. By the time I was in the seventh grade, I had come close to dying from suicide eight times. My aunt, who was my godmother, was the only person I ever felt I could lean on. She was the only one in the world who made me feel loved and wanted. When I was in the eighth grade she was diagnosed with terminal lung cancer. I watched over her and accompanied her as she went through all of her treatments. I witnessed the pain she went through and it broke my heart. But her faith in "God's plan" never faltered.

When she died it almost killed me. I had lost the only form of stable emotional support. I had lost the only person I felt even loved me. But I went on, I was so torn inside, but I had to pick up my mother; she had also lost a best friend and a sister. I felt like I was all that she had left. My god-mother had given me everything and I owed her. My mother needed me and I needed to be there. So I tried my hardest, but I was still broken inside.

I felt worthless; no one told me otherwise. I kept on hurting myself; I thought about killing myself numerous times, but I couldn't leave my mother. And then one night the worst thing could have happened; I heard my parents fighting again, and I knew that I would be the one to get the heat from it, but I didn't expect my mother to come barging into my room telling me that she never saw me helping her, and that I did nothing for her, and that I never would. That hit me so hard, because the only reason I felt I never died or ran away was because I thought that I needed to protect her, and it hurt me so badly that she said that. I cut myself that night, longer and deeper than I ever had before; it was the first time that I used a knife. I let myself bleed, the wounds were so deep, I still have the scars. I went a week not even looking at my mother. I thought about leaving, but I couldn't. And finally, I just broke down. I had a gun pointed at my head, my hand was steady, and all I needed to do was pull the trigger. I closed my eyes, and all of a sudden my mother was in my head, and all of a sudden, all of the anger, heartache, and regret went away. I went home and knew that I couldn't leave. Later I found out that a friend of mine had prayed a Rosary for me and another had gone to Mass for me the same night.

And now I realize and know that everything I went through was meant to strengthen me. In addition to what I just told you, I was raped, beaten, emotionally torn, and I watched the one that I love die, but my life is great. Each hardship made me stronger. My godmother's death brought my mother and me together. All that I've been through is nothing compared to what so many others out there are going through. And I can only hope that my story can help and encourage others, because I'm still alive, and I can't stay silent about that fact!

Justin's Response

You are not the first person to tell me that you wanted to kill yourself. I've heard many youth tell me they wanted to commit suicide. I always ask myself the same questions: Why would they want to destroy such beautiful things? Why would they want to destroy the wonderful smiles, hearts, hands, feet, or even the precious faces that God made?

A friend of our family, named Julie, killed herself. She was twenty years old, her family loved her, and her aunts and uncles cared for her. Everyone wanted to know why she killed herself. Why? Why? How could anyone's life be that bad? She was a really good person!

Even a loving family is not always protection against a hurtful world that can destroy the heart and mind of any human being. You looked for the encouragement you needed from your godmother, and I am sorry to hear that she went home to God. I am sorry to say that a family cannot always protect you.

Many people look for encouragement from others outside their families. That's why it is so important for us to be encouraging to those around us. We never know when that encouragement could save someone's life.

I learned this lesson the hard way. When I was fifteen years old a girl whom I deemed ugly approached me and asked me to dance with her. I said, "Yeah, I would dance with you if you were not so ugly!"

She was crushed. When I saw her four years later she told me, "I wanted to kill myself that night."

I learned to take seriously the words I use and the actions I take every day. We all need to learn that our words and actions are important and can do other people either great good or great harm. Discouragement after discouragement can lead to the destruction of any human.

Your pain didn't come from just your family. It came from other uncontrollable, hurtful experiences, too.

A relationship with God is the answer. To get through this life you can't focus on what people think of you. Instead, focus on what the King of the Universe thinks!

If God is with you all the time, you will persevere through troubled times. If you let God be your encouragement, rather than humans, your family, or outside experiences, then you will never suffer from self-doubt.

A Call to Action!

1. Call someone you care about and ask them what they would think if you killed yourself.
2. See a school guidance counselor ASAP. Talk to your family and to whoever is close to you.
3. Find a community of believers with whom you can hang out.

4. Go eat your favorite snack and think, "I would never be able to eat this again."

5. Go to a retreat at your local church.

6. Write down the following message: *"There is something inside me saying I am worth something. I know who I am. I have a purpose in life. I am not going to listen to lies!"*

7. Find a pastor of a church and share your story. Ask if you could share your story with a youth group. Tell the pastor that others are having similar thoughts and need to be encouraged. We are not alone!

I Am Alone

"I command you: Be firm and steadfast! Do not fear nor be dismayed, for the Lord, your God, is with you wherever you go!" **Jo 1:9**

Dear Minister Fatica,

My family was never very religious. We only went to church on Easter or other holidays, or when we were at my grandparents' house, because they went to church every Sunday, and even some weekdays. They are pretty religious, but my family never followed in their footsteps. I thought that my life was fine. I didn't have too many "tragedies" in my life like the ones that you hear about on TV or something. I was just always a good kid. I always did everything that I was supposed to do. I always got good grades, never got into trouble, and was always nice to people.

The trauma began in seventh grade. I started to fight a lot with my mom, I mean a lot, and with this girl at school who was extremely mean to me. She used to tease me and try to get my friends to ignore me and hang out with her instead. I became very conscious of what everyone thought of me, and I began to really hate myself because I never really got a good response from everyone else. People started to make comments about my looks, personality, "social status," and other things, and it all started to really get to me! I felt like I wasn't loved and that I wasn't good enough!

Then eighth grade came. I was arguing more and more with my mom, and more and more with that girl at school. Eventually, one day at lunch it got way out of hand; I don't even remember what we were arguing about. Anyway, this girl attempted to choke me! I ended up with red marks on my neck for days. I got so mad that I started to become the most negative person. In the middle of the year my grades slipped. I started not to care about anything. I didn't care about school, I got annoyed at all of my friends, and I hated myself so much, so much! I wanted to look different, to be smarter, cooler, and most of all, I wanted to be happier! Nothing seemed to be going right.

I began to want something, anything, to relieve me from the pain. I couldn't find anything that worked. I just kept on getting worse and worse, to the point where I was up in my room considering committing suicide. I was extremely depressed; I needed something. I wanted something or someone to help me. The school year went on. I started to turn to different things. I never did drugs, or drink, or anything like that. Instead, I turned to rap! My favorite artist by the end of eighth grade was Eminem. Now, you might not think that that's so bad, compared to all of the other stories that you hear, but when you blast the songs in your room just to annoy your parents, and you sing all of the words, even the curse words, as loud as you can, it affects you, and pretty badly at that. My favorite thing to do in eighth grade was to make fun of other people in class, especially those who annoyed me. I loved to make them mad, and I went to all extremes to accomplish it. I got my very first detention because I "tormented" a girl from class.

Then I went to high school, and my life completely turned around. At the beginning of the year my religion teacher talked about God and how much He loved each of us in the class! I started to get the feeling that He had an answer, an answer that I was continuously looking for and had never found. That answer was JESUS CHRIST! I started to go to the prayer group that they have once a week, and it was like a gigantic hole was filled inside of me that nothing else could fill! Then I really felt like I was loved, for the first time ever! I gave my life to Christ on November 3, 2004, and I want to live for Him forever!

I started to go on retreats and they all changed my life forever. I am how I am right now, this very second, because of Jesus Christ! Though, like everyone else, I still have struggles and I still sin, now I face my pain through my faith. I have God on my side now, and nothing gets better than that! I am still striving to live my faith, and though it is hard, I couldn't be any happier!

Lord, I pray for everyone who is angry or depressed and doesn't have anything to turn to. Let them know, Lord, that You are there for them, and that You love them just the way that they are. Lord, show them how much You can offer them and help them through their life. Lord, we all need You, Lord, and I pray for anyone going through what I went through, Lord, because I don't want anyone to suffer the way I did. I don't want to go back to that place, and I don't want anyone else to go to that place either. Amen

Justin's Response

Wow! God has really made an impact in your life. I know there are so many people looking for a reason to believe in the Lord. I think you gave so many people hope that there is a reason to believe.

I hope that you can bear witness to your friends, family, and strangers of what an impact the Lord had on your life. Telling others about your life experience will help you to never go back to your old life. Telling others can also help them.

Just today I told a girl at the YMCA what a beautiful gift my wife is, and how when I came to the Lord my wife was the woman I most admired for her love of God. I prayed with the girl at the YMCA, and she was crying because she was touched by my sincerity and truth.

It is so important to share your heart with others. Remember, when you share your heart, share it in a real and powerful way. I am always trying to bear witness, to strike people's hearts so I can help them.

On one occasion a young man named Brian approached me and said, "Check this CD out!" Brian didn't know I was a minister. He thought I was some cool clown.

I said, "Let me check it out, brother. It better be rap."

He said, "Yeah, it's hot. Don't worry."

I started listening to the CD. I knew it was 50 Cent. I said, "Brian, this is hot. I'll pay you five dollars for this CD."

Since the CD was burned, I knew he'd accept the offer. I gave him the five dollars, and he gave me the CD.

Then, suddenly, I broke his CD in half and threw it at him. I said, "You can have the CD and the five dollars." I wanted to make an impression. I wanted to bear witness in a powerful way. I started talking to Brian and let him know that the music he was listening to is hurtful.

A week later I saw Brian again. He said, "I downloaded Cross Movement, a Gospel Rap group, from the Internet." By being intense and sharing my heart, I had made a difference in Brian's life.

Just as I could help others by bearing witness, so you too can help. Never forget the impact you can have on others. God has done great things for you, and now you have to share your experiences. This world needs you and other young ladies to share their experiences, to tell others how God helped them when they were lonely.

I suggest praying for every person who is lonely. Pray that you can help them grow and become witnesses themselves. This is a great ministry. Pray! Pray for your lonely barber or hairstylist. Pray! Pray for your lonely friend or enemy. Pray! Pray for the lonely grocery store clerk or Starbucks worker.

Last year I asked a Starbucks worker, "Do you have any Rice Krispies Treats?"

She said, "No, sorry, sir, we are all out."

I replied, "That sucks. Those are my favorite!"

She looked up at me with a sad face and said, "My life sucks, too."

I looked back at the line behind me, at all those people who hoped that the talkative loudmouth would just finish his order already. But God put it in my heart to pray for the Starbucks worker. With the line full and my heart pounding, I said, "Could I pray for you?"

135

She said, "Sure."

Then I bowed my head and prayed out loud.

In response, she said, "Thank you very much."

Another Starbucks worker, who had overheard, called out, "Would you pray with me, too?"

I hope no one had an important meeting to get to, because I was conducting a healing service for all the lonely people in Starbucks that day.

I let the experience remind me that bearing witness is powerful. Remember that. Remember that the world needs you.

A Call to Action!

1. Don't watch too much TV or play video games. Go outside and play games with other people.

2. Find other people who are lonely and be their encouragement.

3. Talk to everyone in Wal-Mart, Home Depot, or even at the mall. Be courteous and loving to all you meet.

4. Break every CD you own that has a negative message. (Important note: Not all secular music is bad. Some of it is better than Christian music because it can really touch your heart.)

5. Write down five music artists, celebrities, athletes, or famous people. Pray for them daily and write letters to them, encouraging them to change their lives. If youth role models change their lives, the world would be a better place. Their music and shared experiences could have a positive impact on youth, rather than a negative impact.

(My organization, Mega Youth Ministries, has a 50 Cent mission. We have had over five hundred youth write letters to him asking him to change his life.)

I Am Abandoned

I will never forsake you or abandon you. **Heb 13:5**

Dear Justin Fatica,

My whole life I always tried and wanted to be a "good" kid, but somewhere along the line that got messed up. Growing up I always thought that I would have the perfect family, like one that you would see on TV or something, but it didn't turn out to be like that. My parents always used to argue all of the time. I tried to get them to stop, but they just wouldn't have it; they always used to tell me to go up to my room until they were done "discussing," as they used to call it. Eventually they got divorced. I got so upset, and I got into some of the worst stages of depression. My so-called friends tried to get me out of it, so they would pressure me with drinking and smoking, but I always avoided it as much as possible. I used to run to guys to get love.

I thought that if I had a boyfriend then maybe everything would be all right. But apparently I looked for boyfriends too quickly and picked the wrong ones. By the time I was fourteen my virginity had been taken away from me, and I had been molested twice. I kept on going through a lot of depression, and my teachers started to notice so they started to talk to me and try to get me help. One of them suggested that I go to a local youth group, where I could find kids that were going through similar problems. So I went, and ever since I have been trying to live the "good" kid life, and I've been doing a pretty good job so far, thanks to God.

Justin's Response

It has to be hard feeling so abandoned and forsaken. I feel so empty at times when people talk junk about me. I feel empty when I think the whole world is coming down on me.

Remember that we are in this world together. The jerk feels abandoned, and even the nicest person feels abandoned. You are not alone.

Remember that the Lord has, in His hands, all of those who trust in Him. If you can trust in God, you can do anything.

I am so proud to know that you sought the help of other people when you were depressed. That is the key to surviving emptiness.

Where do you go when you feel discouraged? What do you do when you are depressed? Please take twenty minutes every day to pray and ask God for help. Do it right now, before you forget! Ask God to help you know how beautiful and amazing you are.

A Call to Action!

1. Remember, God has the whole world in His hands. Find a group of people who will encourage you.
2. Look at your past and all that you have been through. You got through those rough times. Believe that you can learn

from your past. Ask three people how they got through their rough times.

3. Your actions and mistakes do not make you who you are. You are the magnificent child of God! You are loved! God believes in you and cares for you no matter what! Nothing you do or say about yourself can change that.

4. Go buy a dog chain that reads I AM LOVED NO MATTER WHAT! Don't put any picture on it. If you wear that chain, people will ask you, "What is that dog chain all about?" You will say it reminds you that you are loved no matter what! People will ask you who loves you no matter what. Is it your mom, your girlfriend, or your best friend? You will say, "No. God loves me no matter what!"

5. Ask a friend to write you a letter you can keep between the pages of this book, explaining why you should strive to be a great person. All people are good, because God made them. But you should strive to be great. When you are feeling down, find the letter and read it.

Life Is Nothing Without Him

I say to the Lord, you are my Lord, you are my only good. **Ps 16:2**

Dear Justin,

When I think of how much pain I have gone through, I realize that it is only by God's grace and love that I am still alive.

When I was four I moved forty-five minutes away from the place that I called home. My mother was diagnosed with lupus, Bell's palsy, high cholesterol, and high blood pressure. When I was six, my father's head went through the windshield in a car accident. When I was younger, my uncle molested me on two different occasions, and I was forced to touch him. My father was in the hospital for a while because he had to get bypass surgery. My mother used to hit me when I was little. I lost my best friend of nine years. My other friend died of cancer at the age of sixteen, another one died in the hospital due to malpractice, and another one had two seizures and almost died, while another one drank a bottle of vodka and tried to commit suicide. I have been stalked, threatened, and sexually harassed online by my uncle and boys. People used to make fun of me because of the way I looked. During 9/11 people made fun of me and hurt me because of my ethnicity and my religion. My boyfriend broke up with me after I poured my heart out to him. Boys would date me just to break up with me. I have been treated for chronic migraines with three different medications; so far none of them has worked. My father and my mother almost went through a divorce; they never wear their wedding bands or show any love to each other. My cousin was sent to Iraq to fight. My relatives think that I'm anorexic because I'm a vegetarian. My family is in about nine thousand dollars of debt and has considered filing for bankruptcy. My father lost his job because of his union. I took a recent blood test and I may have anemia.

People tell me that there's no God; I stare back at them with tears in my eyes and tell them, who else could have saved me from all of that pain? Who has ever been through this agony and suffering? Who could ever heal me from these battle scars and wounds? What should I do? Do I have anything but garbage to live for? Will I ever believe?

Justin's Response

So where are you going to go? What happens when you die? If there is no God, then on whom do you rely? If there is no God, then who is first in your life?

What will you live for? There is one thing I have realized. I am nothing without God.

If my family hurts me, where do I go? If my friends hurt me, where do I go? If someone close to me betrays me, where do I go? Do I go to drugs or to friends who may hurt me? Where do I go?

Go to God. God is our only hope. He is our only strength. He is the rock on which we can firmly set our lives. He is our fortress and our refuge. It can't hurt to believe, hope, and have faith in God.

Someone once said to me, "God is opium for the masses." This suggests that God is a fake reality that we made up in order to give us hope in troubled times. I've heard people say, "Humans should be our hope, not something we can't see or feel."

I answer these people by saying, "We should not live for humans because humans make mistakes and let themselves down. But God does not err, and He does not let anyone down.

"Believe in God, the King of the Universe, the Big Daddy, the Father who has the whole world in His hands, who started everything, the Alpha and Omega, the beginning and the end, our Father who wants to develop a personal relationship with you right now. A belief in God, if you hold it firmly and truly in your heart, will bring you peace.

"Believe in having a relationship with Jesus Christ, who has suffered more pain than anyone. Believe in Jesus Christ, who has had problems but who arose again on the third day. This is such a positive belief!

"Why is it so positive? Maybe it is positive because God is real. Maybe He created your heart in such a way that when you please Him, you will get a positive power within you that drives your life above and beyond the call of duty."

COULD ANYONE LOOK YOU IN THE EYE AND SAY THAT BELIEVING THIS IS STUPID?

I say, "No way."

A Call to Action!

1. Write down all the places you have gone that have let you down, and ask yourself if they are worth living for.
2. When you feel like garbage, when you feel that you are worth nothing, what will help you become positive? When you are empty, what can fill you up? If you answer "Nothing," then you can realize that we are nothing without God.
3. Write down how you feel when you believe, with all your heart, that there is a God, a magnificent Lover who cares for you, believes in you, and wants to have a relationship with you forever in Heaven.
4. Write down how you would feel if you believed that there is no God.

I Liked Drugs Before I Met God

They promise them freedom, though they themselves are slaves of corruption, for a person is a slave of whatever overcomes him. **2 Pt 2:19**

Dear Justin,

I was born in the early months of 1990. I was the first-born son to Mary and Anthony. My whole family was so excited and happy. I was the newest addition to the family since 1981. I remember that my grandpa loved me so much. Until I was four I lived with him. Now I feel so bad for lying to my grandfather about who I am. I was the every-day good kid until about seventh grade. I always listened to the classic oldies on the radio, but then I started to get into more psychedelic stuff, like Led Zeppelin, Black Sabbath, and the Doors. All of this music led to my thinking, Maybe I should do drugs. So I tried pot, no big deal right? I realized it was such an unhealthy addiction. I'd do it a few times a week, but in return I could then write music like that, which I came to love. The summer of eighth grade I got hooked on acid. I would do it once a week, and then school came around. I shaved my head; I went from hair down to my shoulders to none.

That was an attempt to get clean, but it didn't really work. Then I met you, and I thought you were the biggest a—— in the whole world. I would mock the kids who said that Fatica changed their lives instantly. I thought that it was all bull. But I learned that it was something that you have to ease into. By November of 2004 I was clean of all drugs and sober from all alcohol. And, even though it sounds crazy, I started to get into God. I'm still in the process, but I'm almost there. The one thing that I regret about pot is that my memory is gone. I hope that it comes back. Now I love Jesus! The thing that I love about Him the most is that I know He'll never judge me. I have a relationship with Jesus and that is one gift that will always be there for me.

Justin's Response

When people ask you, "What are you addicted to?" you can say with a sincere heart, "Jesus is my addiction."

I am so impressed by people like you who can continue on the path of righteousness after facing the addiction and manipulation of drugs.

Remember, you are a slave to whatever you cannot stop. So many people are slaves to negative things, but why not be a slave to the positive power that lives within you? We might not always be able to help others directly, but by encouraging them and loving them we can be an inspiration for them.

Wow! What a difference I could make if I became a slave of Christianity, Jesus Christ, love, peace, patience, kindness, mercy, or believing in what might seem impossible!

Never forget the beauty of these positive addictions and the power that a purposeful addiction can have on your life. But if you have negative addictions, make sure to acknowledge that you have them. Many people are destroyed by addictions they won't acknowledge.

One day I told a friend, "Stop drinking." But he told me that he didn't want to stop, but that he could stop if he wanted to.

"Okay," I told him, "I will pay you one thousand dollars if you don't drink or do drugs for two months." But he wouldn't make that bet because he didn't want to stop.

So I said, "If you really wanted to do drugs and drink, then you would stop for two months, get the thousand dollars, and spend that money on lots of drugs!"

But he just said "Whatever" to me.

If you ever realize you cannot stop, even for two months, then know that you have a problem. If you have negative addictions, acknowledge them and then do something about them.

My grandmother always says, "Everything in moderation." That is a good lesson. Intense addictions to most things, like TV, video games, drinking, or drugs, can destroy families and friendships.

A Call to Action!

1. Write down the names of your friends who have addictions. Pray for them and then write them letters telling them you are going to change your addictions and tell them that you want them to change, too.

2. Talk to the people you know who have had addictions in the past but who have conquered them. Ask them for help to get you out of your problem.

3. Spend time with your grandparents or the elderly and talk to them about your life. Tell them what has happened to you. Visit them and share with them. Don't be afraid to go see them in a nursing home or in the hospital. They are the least likely to judge because they have been through

so much. They will truly be proud of who you are trying to become. Make them feel worthwhile by telling them that they really helped you through your struggles.

4. Visit the homeless and talk to them about your struggles. The greatest time I had was when I took a homeless man to T.G.I. Fridays. The restaurant wanted to kick the homeless man and me out. I poured out my heart to the homeless man, and he helped me through my struggles. And I think that I helped him too!

Family and Pride

"And if my people, upon whom my name has been pronounced, humble themselves and pray, and seek my presence and turn from their evil ways, I will hear them from heaven and pardon their sins and revive their land." **2 Chr 7:14**

Hey Justin,

I can't deal with my family. I really think they don't even want me. I was adopted and I don't know why they even did it. I am so depressed and empty because all of the people in my life don't want me. My parents are divorced, and one parent will throw me out then another one. I just want to be loved, Justin. I just want to be loved. Why do I have to deal with my dad's pride of not wanting to show he is weak and needs help? Why do I have to deal with my sister? When we were kids we used to be able to talk and cry and laugh. Now all we do is fight. I just feel like I am the adopted kid who no one loves.

Justin's Response

You're so beautiful. Thank you for sharing your heart with me.

So many young people feel abandoned by their families. I won't say that it is fair or right. You do not deserve any of the pain you have experienced.

You cannot, however, force your family to change. Remember, you cannot force change.

What can you do? You are the one who can change. You can decide, today, to deal with your family's challenges in a loving way. Jesus could have hung on the cross saying, "Screw all those people who have hurt me." But no! Jesus said, "Forgive them. They know not what they do." Think about that for a second.

You are going to have to deal with your family, right? So why not shock them? Why not love them despite their garbage? Love them. Love them. Love them to the point where it hurts.

Now, I know you are not Jesus, but what if you just tried to do as He did? You are going to feel pain anyway. You are going to have to deal with your family anyway, so deal with them with love and heart. That would be amazing.

Your dad is prideful. Maybe he needs people to share their hearts with him. I remember sitting with my dad, crying real tears with a real heart. My dad got annoyed and said, "Why are you crying? It is not so bad."

I replied, "I am just sharing what I feel!"

Ever since then things have been different. My father really tries to comfort me more and care about my life more. I'm not sure that our talk profoundly changed anything. My father would probably say it didn't. But I know that it affected our relationship in a positive way.

It doesn't matter what effect you have on others. It matters that you share your heart and be real.

A Call to Action!

1. Share your heart but don't expect a reaction. It could be bad or good, but failing to share your heart would be negative.

2. At all costs look for ways you can say you're sorry and work on changing what your family wants you to change. Try your best if your family makes reasonable requests.

3. Pray for your family and believe that God will help you with your struggle. Reach out to people you feel could be role models for your family members. Even if you can't help your family, maybe someone else can.

4. Be weak, not strong. The weak are strong and the strong are weak! Sit down with others—your father, your enemies, or your friends. Share your weaknesses with them. Boast about your weaknesses ten times a day. The people with whom you share will be more apt to listen to you and they may share, too. Do not expect a reaction, though. It takes time.

Fathers Leaving Home

Even if my father and mother forsake me, the Lord
will take me in. **Ps 27:10**

Dear Mr. Fatica,

I always had a good life. I never saw that many struggles,
never really got into too much trouble, and I always had
great friends and did well in school. But then I noticed that
my parents were starting to fight more. I pretended like I
didn't notice, and that it didn't bother me, but it really did. I
wanted to say something, but I just hoped that it was a hard
time in their marriage, and I prayed that it would just go
away, but it didn't. Soon after, it got really bad. They told
me they were getting divorced. That whole time when they
were in court going back and forth seemed like just one big
nightmare. All I could think about was all of the memories
that we had when I was little and growing up, and every
memory had both of them in it, but no more, no more memories, or "Kodak" family moments. I stayed in custody with
my mother, and actually my father moved in next door to
us, so I didn't think that it would be that bad. It seemed like
a different divorce than others I had heard about. My dad
really didn't leave, he just moved next door, and I could go
and visit him anytime I wanted to. But I soon found out that
my mother didn't like that very much, and it just caused
more arguments between them. And since they were right
next door to each other, it seemed like I was in the middle.
My dad eventually moved away, and I really don't see him
too often now. My mom tries to encourage me, but there is
little that she can do. My friends have really helped me the
most. They have the whole Jesus thing going on, and they

are trying to get me hooked, and I have to admit, it's working. Now I pray for my dad, and I am starting to see God as my Father more and more each day.

Justin's Response

My nephews dealt with a situation similar to yours. It pains me to hear their stories. I pray for my nephews often that what they have been through will make them stronger.

I believe that you and my nephews were put in the middle of everything for a reason. I hope you will see that pain is in your life for a reason, so you can better appreciate the Gospel and better help others to live by it.

Perhaps in experiencing pain we can better help both others and ourselves to be happy.

What if my nephews come to me and ask, "Why did Mommy and Daddy get divorced?" First I would tell them, "You need to love your mommy and daddy." Then I would tell them that God allowed the divorce to happen. It wasn't right, but truly God can make your mess a message. Allow God into your life and He will reveal in deeper ways why it happened.

"You were given this pain so that you can use it for good. Do not be mad with your mommy and daddy. Tell them that you love and support them no matter what happens."

I hope that you, too, can approach divorce in a positive way. God will teach you how to get through it. He will give you the wisdom.

As the Psalm says, the Lord will not forsake you or ever leave you. This is a very important lesson to learn. Your grandma, grandpa, nana, papa, mom, dad, little sister or even your big brother will not be with you forever, but a relationship with God, our loving Father, will be there forever.

So if your father has left you, as my nephews' father has left them, know that God will never leave or forsake you. I forgive my brother-in-law, and I am so proud of my nephews for being so loving and caring to their mother, father, stepmother, and stepfather.

But I hope that my nephews and you never forget that no matter who else leaves you or what disagreements happen, you can always count on God. God is the gift that never leaves you. For all of you whose fathers have died or left, remember that you will always have the best gift ever. That gift is God.

Don't give up! He will never give up on you.

A Call to Action!

1. Be a great help to your mother. My nephews have been such a help to my sister. I believe that is one of the major ways my sister has gotten through this. Be a help to your mom, not a burden. She needs you!

2. Find male role models in your life, not to replace your father but to help guide you in life. If you cannot find them for yourself, ask for help.

3. Talk to your family. Ask them about what happened and try to talk through it. Talk with your mom and dad and share your feelings about the situation. You have a right to know and a right to share your heart. Forgive those who have hurt you. As hard as it may be, love your enemies.

4) When you feel and believe that you are healed, write a

letter to your mom and dad. Tell them you understand that life is not easy. Tell them you forgive them and believe in them.

Meaningful Friendships

Your own friend and your father's friend forsake not; but if ruin befalls you, enter not a kinsman's house. Better is a neighbor near at hand than a brother far away. **Prv 27:10**

Dear Justin,

Without one of my friends I would never have recovered from my past. A praying friend has been my key to life. I went through so much pain, but God sent me a friend to shelter me. When I was little my father molested me. He used to come into my room at night while I was sleeping and wake me up and then he would do it. My mother finally divorced him, and she remarried, and now I have a new stepdad. Although I tried to continue living my life, I never really healed. So I hooked up with guys and sought love from them to make myself feel better, and I would look at porn to try to make myself accept my past. But it still hurt. Then one day I met my best friend, and one of the first things she did was pray with me. We talked for hours, and she was the first one I felt comfortable talking to about my past. She prayed over me again for healing, and the tears just came streaming down my cheeks. Ever since that day I have been healed, and I have been motivated to live for Jesus. I have been talking to my mom, and she is helping me get help. And I have been talking to my real dad more and more, and I was finally able to forgive him, and I don't think that my healing was complete until that moment. Only through Christ was I able to do that. Now I am much happier, and Christ is always there to strengthen me.

Justin's Response

It seems that you have found a friend forever. Like Michael W. Smith says, "Friends are friends forever if the Lord is Lord of them." Keep this friend for life and tell this friend how much you appreciate her.

Look for more friends with positive qualities. Try to be a friend to others. Try to be the same kind of friend that your friend is to you. Whenever you feel like you want to go back to porn, hooking up, or thinking about the painful past, please call your friend and ask her to pray for you.

Put a large picture of you and your friend in your room. Believe that God brought this friend to you for a big reason, and never forget what this friend did for you in the past. A faithful friend is a gift not to be taken for granted.

Hold onto your friends tight. Treat them like your fine china. People in the world treat their faithful friends like paper plates. They feel like their friends will be with them forever, no matter how they treat them. Treat your faithful friends like fine china, and your life will prosper greatly.

A Call to Action!

1. Believe that if your friends have changed your life in a positive way, they are friends to keep forever.

2. Spend time listening to your friends. Try to help and encourage them, as they have helped and encouraged you. Change their lives as they have changed yours.

3. Find friends who love you for who you are, not what you play or how cool you are.

4. Write out a plan to develop better friendships.

5. Ken and Brian are probably my best friends. I am confident that even if I lived in Australia, they would strive to keep our friendship going. Focus on friendships like these, friendships that will last forever.

6. It is important to have a core group of friends from your area. I thank God for my friendships in Syracuse and North Jersey.

Lifelong Friendships

He who is a friend is always a friend, and a brother is born for the time of stress. **Prv 17:17**

Dear Justin,

I am so grateful for what Christ has done in my life! I remember all of the pain that I was in because of my dad. When he left me, I felt so lost, so alone, and so empty. My dad and I always had a special connection, and when he left I felt like there was a huge hole formed in my heart. My mother tried to comfort me, but there was little that she could do. I lost all of my self-esteem, and I felt that if he left me, then no one truly loved me. I started to cut myself, and I didn't see any real point in life. I missed him so much, and I was so confused because I still loved him, but at the same time I hated him so much. Then my friends took me to a prayer night that they have at the school, and I slowly began to see that I am loved! I have a Father, a heavenly one who will always love me! I don't know where I would be without those weekly prayer nights. I stopped cutting myself, I got all of my self-esteem back, and I even got to the point where I was able to forgive my father for leaving us, and now I try to pray for him. I pray so much now, I pray for you and your family, for my friends, and for my family. And now my mother and I are in a great relationship because of Christ. Thank you so much for showing Him to me. He has made all the difference! It was because of these great friends whom I hope to have for a lifetime that now I am saved. My life is great because of the amazing friends that the Lord gave me. I hope all can receive the blessing of friends who help you come to Christ.

Justin's Response

As you get older you will realize that your friends can be your family.

If your brothers and sisters are not your friends, try to reach out to them. I, myself, have had a hard time doing this, but I know that establishing positive family relationships is very important to God.

Certainly your friendships could be lifelong relationships, but family is forever. Build a solid foundation with your family. Look to grow a deep, lifelong friendship with your family. This is very important.

It is all the more important because your nephews, nieces, sons, and daughters will be watching your relationships.

How are your relationships with your greatest friends, your brothers, sisters, and mom and dad? Remember that when you get older they are going to be in your life. They will always be with you, so treat them as you would treat those who would give you all the riches in the world. Your relationship with them will be worth more than any amount of money.

"Family" is a funny word. "Family" doesn't always refer to your blood or to the people to whom you are related. "Family" refers to special people in your life. Family cares for you when you are nobody and when you are somebody. Family should be built out of lifelong friendships and sacrifices.

My two great friends, Ken and Brian, are family. I am closer to them than I am to some of my blood relatives. You, too, might be closer to some friends than you are to some of your relatives.

But no matter who makes up your family, you should strive to develop amazing relationships with them. Establish positive relationships with those people who will always help and encourage you.

Dating relationships are often short, while family relationships will last forever. Think before you date someone so that you can decide what type of relationship you want with them.

A Call to Action!

1. Make a list of your lifelong friends. Who are the people you hope will be in your life forever? If you question someone at all, they should not be on your list. Spend time building up your friendships.
2. Talk to your sisters and brothers at least twice a month. Be humble.

The friend responded, "Oh, I don't think [...] girl is pregnant."

I went into my room, sobbing. I cried and cried [...] know what I was going to do. I only saw the girl one [...] that, and she either had an abortion or lied about [...] nancy; there was no baby.

I felt so guilty. How could I have treated anyon[...] Everyone is beautiful. Everyone is a gift fror[...] whole mess with this girl helped me see how [...] beautiful people are, especially when they [...] could I have treated a beautiful gift of Goc[...] gum that you chew up and throw away?

Maybe you've made some mistakes. [...] power to forgive you and to make you p[...] the old and recommit yourself to puri[...] to God.

When I was impure, I thought, "[...] then I learned that I was not being the person [...] to be. I was a beautiful gift of God, and so are you. Now [...] married and have my two beautiful children. I would never want them to give away their hearts, sexuality, or purity to someone who would throw it in the trash like an old piece of gum. I would never want that for my child, and I would never want that for you.

A Call to Action!

1. Share with your potential boyfriend/girlfriend that you do not want to have sex with him or her. Test his or her reactions.

(Middle inserted page)

3. Find ways to encourage your brothers [...] forget to celebrate their birthdays.

4. If you are struggling with a friend, call them [...] them now. Tell them that you are sorry. Talk ou[...] ferences. Commit to a specific time on the phor[...] month or each week. Then make sure you hang out [...] them. Be clear that you don't want to repeat past mista[...] or past arguments. When you and your friend are co[...] mitted to the friendship, move forward in the relationship with your whole heart.

(Right inserted page)

Guarding Your Heart

With closest custody, guard your heart, for in it are the sources of life. **Prv 4:23**

Dear Justin,

You've been teaching me about guarding my heart. But how can I start to guard my heart when it has gone so unprotected for so long? I can't stop thinking of all the times that I've gone below the neck with guys, and how I've allowed them to touch me in all the wrong places. I sit in my bed at night and think about all of them, and tears just start streaming down my cheeks. Then I remember how I lied to my mother about having a boyfriend when she was just trying to talk to me about it. I also remember all of the times that I snuck out of the house to be with my boyfriend for the night. Now that I'm trying to stay pure, my friends don't so much. I want to become pure, and I'm praying for it want to hang out with me anymore, but I will still continue to stay pure. I still feel so dirty, but I'm starting to get a

2. Talk to your potential boyfriend/girlfriend about kissing and tell him or her it is a gift for someone who will not intentionally break your heart. Always share your feelings.

3. Develop dating constraints. Set limits on how long you spend on the phone each night, how many dates you have each week, and what you do on those dates. That way your dating relationship will not get out of control. Think about how you can manage your relationship so that you will never destroy other people's hearts.

Never Put Your Boyfriend or Girlfriend Before Your Family, Friends, or Yourself

"But seek first the kingdom [of God] and his righteousness, and all these things will be given you besides." Mt 6:33

Dear Justin,

You told me that you were worried about me starting a new relationship with someone. Thank you for your worry. I'm worried too. I've made so much progress in my purity, coming from being a sex addict who looked for "love" from every guy I met, to being pure now since I truly dedicated my life to Christ. I'm worried that if I start a new relationship that my purity will get lost too, but I'm a woman of God, and I know now how to guard my heart. I believe that everyone I meet in my life is there for a reason, and I know that there is a reason why God sent me this guy to be in my life. I wasn't even looking for a relationship. I was fine with just Jesus and me. My life is great! And I strive to love Jesus more and more every day. But God sent me

---

Justin's Response

By being honest and heartfelt you are well on ... guarding your heart for the right person. In my heart I kno... that you want to change, and I believe you will succeed. You are sorry, you want to do better, and God sees that your heart is beautiful.

Get on your knees right now and ask God to help you see yourself as precious. You are a gift from God. Know that you are amazing, and believe that you are pure. Once you believe that you are pure, that's what you will focus on. All the other distractions will eventually fade away.

When I was seventeen years old I would take girls to parking lots just to hook up with them. One night when my parents were out of town I gave myself to a girl I barely knew. I felt so bad that night. It was my first time. I had a priest who always used to tell me, "You should be pure. Pray to Mary, because your Mother in Heaven would want you to stay pure."

I immediately apologized to the girl, but the apology felt petty compared to the situation I was in. I felt so terrible that night, and I continued to feel bad over the next week. Then I talked to one of the girl's friends. She told me, "You know, the girl's mother doesn't want her to spend time with you." I said, "I didn't want to be around her anyway, because I don't like her."

someone, and we are both kind of young in our faith, and I know that I will always have a struggle with purity. So as of right now we are very happy just being friends. I like him a lot, and I know that he likes me, but what God wants is more important. Every day when we talk our conversation is based on God, our struggles, the Bible, our opinions, our failures, and our resurrections. Christ is always there. We always try to encourage each other, and I will never tell him everything, because there is a lot saved for my husband. Our relationship is based on the cross. And we make sure that no matter what Christ is the most important to both of us, and we remember that our future spouses are always before us. We also fast from each other during the week so we do not become the number one priority in the other's life. We are excited to pray with each other, and I find that through my relationship with him I am building more trust, because that is something that I have been struggling with. Learning to trust him helps me to trust my friends more, and confide in and respect others more. He is also helping me to turn the knowledge that I have of Christ into living the knowledge. I don't know what plans God has for us, but we are OK being friends for now, and we are setting great goals for guarding our hearts and, most important, guarding Jesus's heart in us if anything should happen.

Justin's Response

Thanks for telling your story with all your heart and soul. You believe that you can do the impossible. That is truly refreshing. You know that while a dating relationship is limited, friendship and family last forever. Never forget that.

I've dated lots of girls. How many of them are still part

of my life? Only one, the one I married. How many friends or family members are still in my life? Over a hundred and that is a fact. And I always remember that God will never leave me.

We should build on the relationships that are most important to us. We should construct our relationship with God, and make that relationship first in our lives. It is essential to put God first, and everything else will follow. Keep your friendships and family strong.

You put the love of Christ first in your life, your family comes next, and then your boyfriend after that. It is a true credit to your Christian beauty that you have the self-control to wait and put other relationships before your relationship with your boyfriend.

You will never let yourself get caught up in the emotional roller coaster of a relationship. You will share the heart-filling warmth of a relationship without experiencing the terrible highs and lows of the roller coaster.

When I was dating my wife she guarded her heart from me so that neither one of us would get hurt. It was really hard but it was so important. She used to let me date her only one night a week. She would let me talk to her for only half an hour a night. She would tell me, "No, I can't hang out because I am too busy."

That hurt me inside. I would say things like, "I guess you don't like me anymore." I would say, "You don't have passion for me, either." But I was just expressing my fleshly desires, and if she had opened up it would have destroyed our relationship.

I believe that my wife and I grew so close because the constraints on our relationship let us keep our priorities straight.

Remember, put God first in your life, everything else second, and your boyfriend third. Then you will have a relationship worth working for.

A Call to Action!

1. Develop constraints on your dating relationship. It is especially important for you to establish rules if you feel you have the lower hand in the relationship (i.e., if you feel like your date could dump you without flinching). Share your heart with your boyfriend/girlfriend, making the rules clear.
2. Focus on friendships and family relationships that are good, structured, and solid.
3. Limit yourself to two dates per week.
4. Schedule phone times when you can talk to your boyfriend/girlfriend. Set a time limit for your phone conversations so they don't take over your entire evening.
5. Find healthy ways to communicate your passions. Find three passions that you share and talk about them. You have a winner if you become excited about the same things.

How to Achieve the Impossible?

Faith is the realization of what is hoped for and evidence of things not seen. **Heb 11:1**

Dear Justin,

I'm fourteen years old and I've gone to a Catholic school pretty much my whole life. My schools really didn't teach me that much about religion, though. They never talked about anything real; we would just take notes and take tests. It was basically just an easy A. But really, life isn't about getting that easy A; life is about happiness. Life is about being joyous through those hard times. But getting back to my life, in seventh grade things got really tough for me. The girls in my class were very mean; they used to talk about me and just try to hurt me in every way possible. They would just talk about me all of the time, and it hurt, but it also made me stronger.

Then my sister went with her boyfriend to California. He was moving there, and she wanted to help him move in. She found out that he was cheating on her, and she got so upset that she threw herself out a seventh-story window. This was terribly painful for my whole family; it was a miracle that she survived. Her guardian angel was definitely looking out for her. She broke two legs, one arm, and she had blood in her lungs because of the big drop. She was in a wheelchair for four months.

My father went to get her from California, and for the next few months we went from hospital to hospital looking for both physical and mental therapy. Just seeing all the pain she went through was almost unbearable for our family. But at least we found out about her depression and could get her some treatment.

Then one day she asked me to help her stand up, and before I knew it she was walking! It was definitely a miracle. She went to therapy five times a week, which helped tremendously. Before we knew it, she was living a normal life again. Now she is doing great, she's my best friend, she's going to college, she has a job, and everything has been amazing.

My sister has been an amazing miracle for all of us in the family; we see now that God has a huge mission for her. She got a second chance to live, and we thank God for her life every day. After this experience my belief in God increased tremendously. Now it is my goal to turn religion class and religion in general into more than just an easy A; I want it to be a lifelong journey.

I started to help out in my youth ministry more, and I think that I started to make a difference. I started to make a lot more friends in school, and I didn't have as much trouble with the other girls as I used to. Now I have friends that are like sisters to me. Now I am a great person, not just good, but great, and I'm in a religion class that is filled with love, joy, and happiness. And it's not such an easy A. I'm encouraged to live my faith more and more each day, and not so long ago, I gave my life to Christ for the first time, and forever! God is everything to me, and He is always there for me. He gave me a great life, with great family and great friends.

Justin's Response

The story about your sister is amazing. Her recovery is a miracle. You have given me the belief and faith that miracles do happen. You have given me faith that miracles can happen to everyday people like you and me.

You have given me hope that my impossible goals can be achieved. Your story has helped me to believe in God's power, and because I believe in God, I receive so many gifts. You, too, have believed and you, too, have received. Have you ever dreamed big and heard everyone say, "No way"? God can grant you the grace to succeed. Did you ever have a problem and say, "I can never get through this"? Know that you can receive God's abundant blessings.

When an obstacle comes at you or me, through prayer and faith we can do the impossible. "Everything is possible to one who has faith" (Mark 9:23).

Remember, you are not an average young lady. You are a GREAT, MIRACULOUS WORK OF GOD'S CREATION! You are loved so magnificently that you have the ability to do anything you want with the power and love of God.

A Call to Action!

1. Write down five things that you think are impossible, for instance, a straight-A report card, writing a book, loving your mother, forgiving a friend . . . Pray that you can achieve the impossible.

2. Pray daily, saying, "For your glory, Lord, help me do something no one thinks I can do."

3. Write down the names of three people no one thinks can change. Pray with all your heart that God can use you to change their lives. Pray for those people and strive to believe in them.

4. THINK BIG! Think out of the box! Think like God would think! Start to dream big and ask God to reveal what He wants you to do. When you find out what you should do, don't rest until you do it. God will bless you for your faith. People say, "Seeing is believing." The Bible says, "Blest are those who believe and do not see."

Build a Team as Jesus Did

"The harvest is abundant but the laborers are few;
so ask the master of the harvest to send out laborers
for his harvest." **Mt 9:37–38**

Dear Justin,

I was challenged this year to bring someone to Christ as a Christmas present. I've been living for Christ full throttle for a while now, so I took up this challenge right away. I targeted my two friends. One of them hurt God really bad; she never told me what it was she did, but she always thought that it was awful, and that God would never forgive her for it. I knew that she needed healing from that and that she needed to be forgiven, so I took her to one of the prayer nights that we had at our school. It was definitely the best night to take her! We had a healing service, and all of those who were hurt went up, and my friend got up and said that she believed that God wouldn't forgive her and then the whole congregation prayed over her, and I could see the change immediately! The rest of the night she was praising and worshiping with her whole heart. She truly believed that she had been forgiven!

My other friend was feeling really alone, like there was no one there for her. She said that Christmas made her sad because it made her remember all of the bad times and the pain that she has had in her life. Looking back she realized there was never anyone there for her along the way. One day I told her that God was there, and that He would always be there for her. She seemed to brush off my comment, but the other day I was reading her profile, and it said that when no one was there, God was there. She seemed a lot happier the next few days, and she said that it was one of the best Christmases she'd had in a while! Now the two of them are still living out their faith and growing deeper everyday!

Justin's Response

AMAZING! I am impressed that you had the courage to share your heart with your friends.

You know a great truth: believe in God's grace and you will receive the harvest. The Lord's abundant blessing is the greatest gift anyone can receive.

I am so impressed by what you have told me. Now, go out and build a team of believers. You have already built a team of three, and this is a great start. But never forget that there are many people who need the love of Jesus!

Keep up the great work of the Lord. I am so impressed when young people go out into the world believing in the impossible. You have experienced one of the greatest achievements in life. You worked to build relationships with Jesus Christ.

Many young people are praised for their skills in sports, for having attractive girlfriends or boyfriends, and for getting good grades. But helping others improve themselves is so much more important!

Continue to focus on encouraging everyone's gifts. Take time to thank God for the people in your life, and really appreciate those people for who they are. There are many people who are not your friends or family members. They could be your enemies, they could be on a different sport team, or maybe they work for a company you don't like. Whoever they are and whatever they do, you should believe in them! Strengthen them as you strengthened your friends. Make them part of your team!

The greatest compliment I could ever receive is: "You totally disagree with the people with whom you work. But still, you make a great team. How do you do it?"

A Call to Action!

1. Find a few people with whom you are close and spend time with them on a regular basis.
2. Find a group of people who are different but have the same mission and vision. Take them out to eat and tell them that you are building a team to help people. Invite them to join you.
3. Then ask each of them to bring five people each to a prayer program each month. Tell them, "Go to the ends of the earth, proclaiming the love of God! Working together is the only way to go!"

What If I Had Never Met the People Who Taught Me So Much?

Command and teach these things. Let no one have contempt for your youth, but set an example for those who believe, in speech, conduct, love, faith, and purity. **1 Tm 4:11–12**

Dear Fatica,

I grew up in a Christian family household, respecting my parents, family, teachers, and myself. I went to Mass every Sunday, and was a part of the Mustard Seed Choir until about sixth grade. It was then that I started to get into trouble. It doesn't sound like any big deal now, but it was a big deal then. It was little things like chewing gum, wearing nail polish, and being out of dress code in a Catholic school. I became very involved in dance. I lived it—ballet, tap, jazz—I would practice every day, and I strove and challenged myself to the extreme to be the best that I could be. Dancing took over Mass on Sundays, and I got to the point where I went on Holidays or Holy Days, but that was really it. I started to get into more fights with my parents because my grades were dropping, and I started to get into many catfights at school with my friends.

As eighth grade came around, I pushed myself at dance more than ever because I was injured over the summer, so I had to get back up to speed. I pushed myself so much I started to go crazy; dancing was all that I could focus on, and all I really cared about. I always felt like I was never good enough for my parents, no matter what grades I got, and on top of that, I got boy crazy, and my friends always got mad because they said I had no time for them anymore. I started to get into a lot of despair, and I often cried myself to sleep at night. It got so bad that I started to cut myself and think about suicide. One day I just broke down. It was during gym class, and I ran into the bathroom and cut myself like crazy. My teacher came in and saw my arms covered with scratches and blood and took me to the office. There I cried for a good two periods. I was forced to talk to my guidance counselor, but it helped more than I expected. I told her everything that was going on in my life, and how I felt. Cutting was a big mistake, now that I think about it.

Everyone started to find out at school, dance, and home, and everyone started to watch out for me.

Then I went to high school, a Catholic one, and I got a new start with new people who didn't know who I was in the past. I had religion my first period class, and I really started to listen to the lessons, and I admired you, my teacher, for your enthusiasm and love for Christ. I learned a lot, and I realized that God does really love me, and the Bible is an amazing book.

Romans 8:28 says that all things work for good for those who love the Lord, who are called according to His purpose. This is my favorite verse because it gives me so much hope, and it reminds me of when I dedicated my life to Christ on December 22, 2004, right before Christmas! I believe that I am strong and am growing successfully in my faith, and my life has started to come together piece by piece. I am so very pleased to have discovered God's love, and I thank Him for all the opportunities that He gives me every day, days past, and days to come; and most important for the fact that He sent His only Son to die for us, so that I could have eternal life. I love you Christ!

Justin's Response

I am confident that I wouldn't be the man I am today without the great people who have been such an important part of my life. I gladly say, in the most humble way I can, "I am Justin Fatica, a man of faith. I believe that the man I am becoming is possible because of all of those people who believed in me. They put their hearts into what matters most to me, Jesus Christ. They believed in me no matter what and they challenged me no matter who I thought I was."

Through the years, many wonderful people have spent countless hours with me. Each person, in his own way, has encouraged me, challenged me, and helped me. Each one has supported me in the most magnificent walk of love a man on earth could imagine.

The least I could do for you is share the love of Christ that so many people have shared with me. It is now your turn to be the person who shares the love. You and I have received so much, and now it is time for us to give back! So many wonderful people have given me the benefit of the doubt. They believed in me. They believed that I am a sincere child of God striving to bring others to Christ in a world that criticizes ministers and people of faith.

Everyone reading my book . . . I sit here in tears writing to all of you. I challenge each of you to call someone who has touched your life and say, "Thank you." Don't be bashful. Take out your phone and call. Call people who loved you and cared about your faith, and tell them you appreciate them.

A Call to Action!

1. Ask random people to be part of your team, to help in building a solid faith in Christ. Write down their names. It's important for you to reach out to others so that you are always meeting new people and through those relationships you will grow in your love for Jesus and for the people who surround you.

2. Ask the person who disagrees with you the most to be part of your life. Sometimes the relationships that we struggle with the most are the ones that make us strong and chal-

lenge us. Write down the person's name and call him or her today.

3. Call the people in your life who really annoy you and hang out with them. Tell them how amazing their gifts are and please remember to be sincere. By extending yourself and by giving those you know the least your love, you are growing in God's love as well.

Afterword by Father Larry Richards

I first met Justin when he was a junior in the theology class I taught at Cathedral Preparatory High School for boys in Erie, Pennsylvania. He was a smart-aleck from the beginning, always trying to be funny and give me a hard time. He always thought he knew more than anyone else and was always very sarcastic with me, but that changed after he met Jesus.

I really had no idea how Justin would respond when I asked him to attend a religious retreat that we were having the next weekend. But I needed to try to open his eyes to the power of God's love; I had no idea how he would respond. I thought that given his unpredictability, there was a very good chance that he would reject what God wanted him to do. I was bringing a new retreat movement into the Diocese called Teens Encounter Christ (TEC), and I was praying about who to invite. The Lord kept bringing to my mind that I should invite Justin and I kept rejecting that thought because, honestly, I could not stand Justin at the time.

Finally the Lord prevailed upon me and I told Him, "Well, I will invite him, but he won't come!" So the next day I invited Justin to come to our first TEC retreat and sure enough he told me: "No, I am not coming. I already know Jesus, Father!" And I said to him, "Well, if you do come then you can show Him to us!" and so, of course, he came. It was during that TEC retreat that Justin came to know that Jesus Christ was alive and that he wanted a relationship with Him.

Whenever I am faced with challenging students, I pray for them. I follow what Jesus said: "Love your enemies, pray for those who persecute you." Justin was the one student I liked the least and so I put him on my prayer list and started to pray for him each day; that was how the Lord started to work on my heart toward Justin. It was through this prayer and God's grace that God worked a miracle of love in my life toward Justin and in Justin's life toward God.

With the Hard as Nails Ministries Justin has found a way to reach out to young people in a loud and intense way that they respond to. My style of ministry is very similar to Justin's, just not as "in your face." Well, maybe just a little "in your face," but not as intense usually. Justin's ministry reaches out to those who need Jesus the most, the ones you will not find in our churches on Sundays, and that is why his ministry is so needed. Controversy, the type that Justin sometimes experiences, arises from those who are easily offended, and some people are just looking to be offended.

Justin loves those kids and he loves Jesus Christ. Jesus said: "You will be hated by all because of my name" (Lk 21:17). Justin just wants to bring people to Christ; he will not be able to reach everyone, but the ones that Jesus wants him to touch will hear his message. Each of the apostles were very different and God used each in a special way, so it is with Justin. We need to rejoice that he can reach youth that many people cannot.

Justin talks a lot about bringing the youth back to the Catholic Church because they are the future; Hard as Nails Ministries is just one of the ways to make this happen. Above all else, we need to pray for them. I mean committed daily prayer for the youth we know by name. When we pray for someone it is like rays of sun shining through a magnifying glass—it sets them on fire! When we pray we become a human magnifying glass and we place ourselves spiritually over the person we pray for, and the Grace of God, which is like the rays of the sun, is focused through us, and then the Holy Spirit can set them on fire with His love.

The second thing that we need to do is love them. We need to love our youth with the pure love of God! This happens best when we get out of the way and let God love others through us. People will not listen to us unless they know that we love them and want what is best for them—not for us!

Finally, we've got to show them by the way we live. I once got Justin a plaque that had one of my favorite sayings of Saint Francis on it: "Preach the Gospel at all times and IF NECESSARY use words!" We need to love first because if we don't do that, no one will believe us when we tell them about God's love. There is a song verse that reads: "Don't tell them Jesus loves them until you're ready to love them, too!" Justin loves the youth that he ministers to and so must we.

Justin and I have a strong, supportive relationship because we both have the same goal, "To bring the world to Jesus Christ!" Because we are very much alike we can continue to challenge each other to grow more in love with Jesus each day and also to encourage each other when the world is turning against us. Jesus never sent out Lone Rangers—He always sent them out two by two so that they could support each other and encourage each other to always do God's will. Justin and I have always made time for each other so that we can be all that God is calling us to be.

I am very hopeful for the future of the Church. The image that I like to use is that I think that the Church is pregnant right now and we are on the verge of a new evangelization. I think that there are some tough times awaiting us, and that is why we need ministries like Justin's that are helping to make people strong so that we can endure whatever is coming. We know that all things will work together for good and that we are within the Will of God; we know that He will never let us go! More and more laypeople like Justin are rising up in faithful leadership in the Catholic Church, and God is using them to bring more and more people to the knowledge of the Truth. I am very excited about where God is leading us all!

Father Larry Richards is the founder of The Reason for Our Hope foundation (www.thereasonforourhope.org) and he is the pastor of St. Joseph's Church in Erie, Pennsylvania. He travels throughout the country as a nationally recognized Catholic speaker. Father Larry was also Justin's eleventh-grade theology teacher at Cathedral Preparatory School in Erie, Pennsylvania.

Acknowledgments

There are so many people who have helped me in the process of writing this book. I would like to thank those who have given me inspiration, who have believed in the Hard as Nails mission since day one and who have advised and given me wisdom and will continue to in the future.

First and foremost, I would like to thank my editor at Doubleday, Trace Murphy, who gave me the opportunity to tell my story. His support has been an inspiration to me. I would also like to thank Darya Porat, who worked as the assistant editor on this project. The enthusiasm of the terrific marketing team of Mara Lander and Julie Sills has been so encouraging to me and I thank them immensely. Thanks also to everyone at Doubleday who worked on the development and publication of this book.

Cathy Hemming, my agent, made this miracle possible. Thanks also to Andrew Corsa, who believed in this book and the idea from the very beginning.

I would like to thank Sheryl Stebbins, one of the most amazing women I have ever met. Without Sheryl this book would not have been possible. She gave hours upon hours of her time to make this book what it is today. On a more personal note, Sheryl has become a very special friend to me. Her encouragement through the process of writing this book has been invaluable. Her consistent selflessness has given me an incredible example to live up to and I am sure that her kindness has brought me and many others to know the love of God in a new and important way. There are few people on this earth who would do what Sheryl has done, and I will be forever grateful for the blessing of knowing her.

I am grateful to Father Larry Richards for writing an inspiring Afterword. David Tyree, who has become a personal friend, was so kind to write the Foreword to encourage others that no matter what we have been through we can all live for Christ.

I would like to also thank my wife, Mary, and our children, Joseph and Catherine, who inspire me everyday to continue writing books that will impact the world in positive ways. And also my father, Jack Fatica, who pushes me to be the best man that I can be and my mother, Kathleen Fatica, for her constant love and support. I thank my whole family who have instilled the never-doubting attitude in my heart through their passionate love for me.

I would like to thank everyone who has supported my mission to write this book; they have believed in this project and have encouraged me through the entire process:

Nancy Abraham, Arian Agadi, Ravi Agadi, Priyanka Agadi, Sarita Agadi, Father Lou Aiello, Rocky Balboa, Ashley Begay, Amy Boutcher, Danny Boutcher, Monsignor William Biebel, Danny Buggs, Rick Burslam, Vicki Burslam, Barbara Camp, Melissa Campbell, TJ Churchill, Tom Churchill,

Bishop Thomas J. Costello, John Cowlin, Brian Craven, Rachael Dalo, Caroline Gambale Dirkes, Dan Dirkes, Father Michael Donovan, Joseph "Whisper" Dowdy, Patti Dugan, Michele Evanson, Corey Ferraro, JC Fatica, Jeff Fatica, Jeff Galletly, Joni Galletly, Robert Galletly, Stacey Galletly, Christina Gasparini, Brian Greenfield, Genevieve Greenfield, Dave Groesbeck, Father John Fenlon, Alisha Frawls, Brian Haghighi, Bob Halligan Jr., Linda Halligan, Tim Hanley, Michael Henty, David Holbrooke, Sarah Holbrooke, Paul Houlis, Eileen Iannuzzi, Megan Iannuzzi, Craig Jandoli, Jack Jones, Mary Jones, Doreen Jones, Ichiro Kawasaki, Natasha Kawasaki, Erin Kelly, Ricky Kharos, Sarah Klein, Father Bryan Lang, Barbara LaPorte, Joseph LaPorte, Matthew LaPorte, Priscilla LaPorte, Jim Leana, Sandy Leana, Ed Leon, Bernadette Lysaught, John Lysaught, Caitlin Lundy, Holland Mack, Jessica Manzi, Bishop Salvatore Matano, Mega Youth Ministry, Adam Miller, Ian Miller, Jack Miller, Natalie Fatica Miller, Melissa Mirkovich, Ivan Mills, Rufus Morris, John Murphy, Dan Murray, Maria Murray, Amy Nelson, Ken Nelson, Father Tom Nydegger, the Pace family, the Pachella family, Don Patsy, Karl Patterman, Father Bryan Page, Father Joseph Philips, Father Henry Pedzich, Brian Pedraza, Colin Ranus, RJ Ranus, Father Willy Raymond, Father Peter Reddick, Annette Renaud, Elizabeth Reyes, Mike Rose, Kathleen Sciame, Greg Schlueter, Stephanie Schlueter, Monsignor Robert Sheeran, Fr. Bill Sheridan, Ron Sparagoski, Peter Speech, Auntie Em Sertz, Uncle Ron Sertz, Father James Spera, Rob Spizla, the Tomesco family, Brother Agostino Torres, Twelve Apostles at SHU, Bishop Donald Trautman, Lucy Udell, Jeff Udell, James P. Vail, Colette Vail, Tiffany Vezina, Mick Walker,

Jake Walter, Bob Walters, Young Apostles at PC, Beth Zimmerman, Eric Zimmerman, Gary Zimmerman, Leslie Drewes Zimmerman, Mark Zimmerman, Paul Zimmerman, and the entire Fatica and Iverson families, with special thanks to the Funday crew.

I beg the forgiveness of all those people who have been with me over the years and whose names I have failed to mention here. Thank you for everything!

I would also like to thank the leaders involved with the 12 Apostles program and the students of Paramus Catholic in Paramus, New Jersey, where this all began. To each and every student out there, I truly appreciate all you have done to make this possible.

I thank the hundreds of churches and organizations who have supported Hard as Nails and also the hundreds of thousands of people I have spoken to in person who have experienced the Hard as Nails message. I truly thank everyone who has been inspired around the world through our various media projects.

But nothing is possible without the unconditional love of God and His beloved son, Jesus Christ, which is what motivated me to write this book. By working together in the name of their love and by helping others to achieve their dreams, everything is possible. I truly believe the mission of Hard as Nails and the future of the church is going to happen with the body of Christ saying yes. I am one man and can do nothing alone.

Visit www.doubleday.com/justinfatica and enter the pass-
word JFatica09 for a free download of the song "Love No
Matter What," written by Bob Halligan Jr. and Justin Fatica.

"God loves everyone. He loves unconditionally, and, if we are
truly Christians, then we should do the same. This song challenges us to care equally for all people. The song touches our
hearts and transcends all ethnicities, attitudes, and beliefs.
We must always remember that God loves us no matter what.
He believes in us no matter what. He encourages us no matter what we say."

—Justin Fatica

www.justinfatica.net

The HBO® documentary, *Hard as Nails*, is now available on DVD.